Original Voices

Homeless and Formerly Homeless Women's Writings

By the Women of Mary's Place

Empowering homeless women, children and
families to reclaim their lives

———————————

Book proceeds will benefit women and
writing at Mary's Place.

Original Voices: Homeless and Formerly Homeless
Women's Writings

By the Women of Mary's Place

Edited by Julie Gardner

ISBN: 978-0692645468

Book design: Ginny Booker, Columbia, MO

Original painting, "The Forest," by Diana Balgaard,
Seattle, used with permission on the book cover.

Photograpy: Colleen McDevitt, Seattle

Original Voices gracefully communicates the experience of a community of women who, far too often, remain invisible and unvalued. This simple and vibrant creation speaks to the power and brilliance of the individual voice, regardless of life circumstances. Julie Gardner allows us to sojourn into the circle of love and sisterhood she created when she chose to sit beside a group of women who were once strangers to her.

– **Mary Tuchscherer**, editor *Nda Ku Ona: I See You With My Heart*, and Founder and CEO, VoiceFlame, Inc.

These short first draft writings written in four to twelve minutes by the women at Mary's Place are an opening for readers to see their struggles, imaginations and successes. More significantly, we hear the voices of homeless and formerly homeless women – in their own words.

– **Ingrid Ricks**, author *New York Times* bestseller *Hippie Boy: A Girl's Story* and Founder, Write It Out Loud

The first time I walked into Mary's Place, I knew I'd found one of those special places where people can exhale and really be themselves in the safety of good company and the warmth of kind attention. There is a spirit that fills those rooms - a spirit that embodies the heart, passion, and wild experiences these women carry with them. Julie Gardner has helped to capture that courageous spirit in the pages of *Original Voices*. I am so grateful to have an anthology that carries these words beyond the walls of Mary's Place and out into the world where they can resonate fully.

– **Marya Sea Kaminski**, writer/director, Associate Artistic Director of Seattle Repertory Theatre

What a fine, honest, heart-filled collection of writings by the women of Mary's Place! As Janet Backster writes in her good piece, "Blessing," "May you who wander / never be lost / and in the moment / be-knowing / you will always find your way / our way...." This anthology is a testament to women finding their way by putting their voices on paper in a safe, encouraging writing environment. These women's voices are not only worthy of the page but also powerful, important ones for all to hear.

–**Jan Haag**, author, *Companion Spirit*, and Amherst Writers & Artists affiliate and instructor, and Journalism, English and Creative Writing Professor, Sacramento, CA

This book is dedicated to all women
at Mary's Place and elsewhere
who are homeless or
formerly homeless.

May your voices be heard
and may your stories be told
with love and truth
inviting others to love and truth.

CONTENTS

Foreword, Pat Schneider · *xiii*

Introduction
    About Mary's Place, Marty Hartman · *xviii*

    My Mary's Place Story, Julie Gardner · *xix*

    About The Write to Heal and Have Fun!
    Wednesday Morning Workshop · *xx*

    About This Book · *xxii*

Anne B
    I am a Phenomenal Woman · *1*

Leah
    My Grandmother · *2*

Beth
    Never Liked, Always Liked · *4*
    If I Had Only Four or Five Lines Worth of Ink or Time Left · *5*

Mary Ann
    Never Liked, Always Liked · *6*

Marceline Jackson
    Never Liked, Always Liked · *7*
    If I Had Only Four or Five Lines Worth of Ink or Time Left · *8*
    Cherry · *9*
    Rain Moves Over · *10*
    Dove · *11*
    Patchwork Altar Cloth · *12*

M. J.
    Mean People Suck · *13*

M. R.
    Oh Wondrous Day · *14*
    Starbursting · *15*

Diana Balgaard
    She · *16*
    Her Body Moved · *17*
    Silence · *18*
    Meditation · *19*
    Aztec Indian · *20*
    I Can't Elope · *21*
    Blessing · *22*
    What I Need Today · *23*
    The Moon with Dimples · *24*
    Paper · *25*

Angela Lugo
    My Mary's Place Story · *26*
    Oh Mary, Oh Mary · *27*
    Childhood · *28*
    I Need Turquoise · *29*
    Through All the Gold · *30*

Karli
    Exit 17 · *31*
    Remember You're Here · *32*
    From the Time I Woke Until Now · *33*
    I Don't Have Many Memories · *34*
    My Mom Was a Drunk: True Story · *35*

Elsie
    Once Upon a Time · *36*
    Lust is… · *37*
    The Stick of Wood · *38*

Jennifer Hamilton
    Quaking Aspen Leaves · *39*

Maria
    Alpha (and) Omega · *40*
    I Walked the Green Mile… · *41*

Janet Backster
    The Past, Present and the Future Walked into a Bar · *42*
    J. P. Patches · *43*
    Blue Notes · *44*
    Blessing · *45*
    At Sixteen · *46*
    Wish I Could Just Be Me · *47*
    Dust Poem · *48*
    Richard Bach · *49*
    A Flower in January · *50*
    I Felt the Pores · *51*

Renegade Amazon
    Eulogy for the Fallen Women in Black · *52*

Sue Johnson
    I am Unlearning · *53*
    In the Direction of the Sun · *54*
    Achiever, Man of Worlds · *55*
    Notre Dame de Paris · *56*
    My Intention · *57*
    The New Year is Coming to an End · *58*

Tiffany
    You are What You Eat · *59*
    My Name · *60*

Victoria
    Thank God for Smashed Plums · *61*
    Where I Lived as a Child · *62*
    The Taj Mahal · *63*

Pee Wee
    Four Tools I Can't Live Without · *64*

Kristine Bagby
    Men, Men, Men · *65*
    Joy · *66*
    There are Many Artists · *67*
    Hands · *68*
    Cell Phones · *69*
    A Drive Down the Scenic Back Road · *70*

Pamela Herod
    My Grandmother Told Me · 71
    Walking and Speaking With The Lord · 72
    Since I've Been With The Lord · 73
    After Getting Out of a Relationship with Domestic Violence · 74

Little Bit
    My Eyes are Gone, *A Psalm* · 75
    I Hope the Stars Drip Down, *A Psalm* · 76

Anonymous
    Oh Lord, I Love You, *A Psalm* · 77

Avalon
    How Long God of Mercy?, *A Psalm* · 78
    You are my Rock, *A Psalm* · 79

Debra
    How Long Oh Dear Jesus?, *A Psalm* · 80

Sweet Justice
    Justice Keeper, *A Psalm* · 81
    You are My Stability, *A Psalm* · 82
    How Long Oh Protector?, *A Psalm* · 83

Diana Balgaard
    Yeshua, *A Psalm* · 84
    You are My Rock, *A Psalm* · 85

Anonymous
    Everyone Knew · 86

Hannah
    When I Was Young · 87
    There was an Explorer · 88

Mary
    Making Strangers · 89

Myrna
    As I Write I Create Myself · 90

A.
    Home · 91

Tonya
    Willingness · *92*

Brookland
    Scars · *93*

Kate
    Decisions (Major) · *94*

Anonynmous
    Camp Long · 95

Selppa
    Apples · *96*

Jessica Jo Wood
    The Attic · *97*
    Strawberries and Apricots · *98*
    The Patio · *99*
    Bread Table · *100*

Ms. Helena Rai
    Wars Have Begun and Ended at this Table · *101*

Carla D.
    Attic · *102*
    Resilience · *103*

Red Rock
    The Music · *104*
    Goodbye · *105*
    The Picture · *106*

Myrtle "penny"
    I Go Down to the Edge of · *107*
    Campfire · *108*
    My Own Fall Song · *109*
    Home made Resume · *110*

LJ
    My Immortal Love · *112*
    Thanks to New Beginnings in My Life · *113*
    My Hands · *114*
    Blanket · *115*

Kathryn
   A Window · *116*

K. O.
   Story from a Story · *117*
   A Man Gave Me a Dog · *118*
   My No Good Terrible Bad Dog · *119*

Beebe Berhe
   Baby Blanket · *120*
   It Goes Away · *121*
   I Was Born into a Big World · *122*

Little Bit
   Life Is · *123*
   Dear Reader · *124*
   In Another Life · *125*

Jennifer Hamilton
   For So Long I Did Not Have a Voice · *127*

Acknowledgements · *128*

Appendix
   Our Editing and Decision Making Process · *130*
   About Amherst Writers & Artists · *131*

FOREWORD

When I was eleven years old, my mother moved my younger brother, Sam, and me away from a neighborhood of low-income apartments in St. Louis. We moved into one room in a basement on Pine Street, a quiet street, neat, with tree-shadowed bricks and lawns. Surely a better neighborhood. Surely a better school.

But the one room was dark. There were two small, rectangular windows next to the low ceiling. They let in a little light, but all I could see through them was the grass of the yard. Strangely disorienting, seeing grass above your head. There were two bare light bulbs hanging from the ceiling, one on each side of a coal stove in the center of the room. There was a free-standing sink and an electric heating plate with two burners. There was one bed for the three of us. The door between our room and the rest of the basement was loose; dust from the open coal bin on the other side of the door drifted easily into our room.

One day, when we had been there for a while, the woman from upstairs who owned the home came down and pounded on the door. Mama opened it. As Sam and I looked on, she raged: "Get out! Get out! You have brought roaches into our home! You are filthy! Get out of our house – NOW!"

It was probably true; roaches were rampant in the tenement we had fled. And Mama didn't know how to keep order. Nor did she have the time or the energy. She worked twelve-hour night shifts sitting by the bedside of dying patients. We were "filthy." And at ages eleven and nine, Sam and I believed her – and were ashamed.

We were all homeless. Mama put us into an orphanage.

There are many reasons why a woman might become homeless. Who she is, where she came from, what her stories are, vary across all of our differences, level of education, original privilege or lack of it, color, sexual orientation, age, mental capacity, and on and on. What the writers, with a few exceptions, in this book have in common is the fact of homelessness – now, or in the past.

What they have done in *Original Voices* is break silence. Approximately fifty women, homeless or formerly homeless, with a few exceptions, writing in small groups at Mary's Place give us words – portals into their lives and their imaginations. From some of them we have only a tiny cameo – a glimpse of their inner and/or outer lives. Silence, for some of these writers, is still too great a defense, too deep a survival technique, to allow us to hear the rich, beautifully nuanced voices they would have if they were sitting at their own kitchen tables telling a close friend their stories. The listener would laugh, cry, be moved to outrage, stirred to anger or to celebration, and return story for story. The language would flow like a deep and beautiful river. Some of these writers have been able to give us more. There are rivers here; there are eddies, rapids, still pools. It is for us, the readers, to guess the depth and dimension of experience, the intelligence and wisdom, the originality and diversity of language that flows underneath these glimpses of sun, shadow, and danger.

In her invitation to me to write this introduction, Julie Gardner quoted something I wrote in my book, *Writing Alone and With Others*, (Oxford University Press, 2003). She added, "If you simply can't fit another thing into your schedule, I will have another person write the foreword but I would ask for your blessing to use some of the below."

"The below" is this:

A Writer is someone who writes. Everyone is a writer. You are a writer. All over the world, in every culture, human beings have carved into stone, written on parchment, birch bark, or scraps of paper, and sealed into letters – their words. Those who do not write stories and poems on solid surfaces tell them, sing them, and in so doing, write them on the air. Creating with words is our continuing passion. We dream stories; we make up stories, poems, songs, and tell them to ourselves. All alone, we write. We also write with others. Every time we open our door at the end of a workday and say, "You'll never believe what that [bleep] said to me today…," we create story. "I was minding my own business, and he got right into my face! And then he said…." Already we are creating character, voice, suspense – story. It may not be committed to paper, but the artist, the writer is at work.

We are all connected to one another and to the mystery of the universe through our strange and marvelous ability to create words. When we write, we create, and when we offer our creation to one another, we close the wounds of loneliness and may participate in healing the broken world. Our words, our truth, our imagining, our dreaming, may be the best gifts we have to give.

Original Voices is a collection of writings unlike those we usually read. To read here is to be given the privilege of hearing intimate voices of homeless or formerly homeless women, sometimes grieving, sometimes sharing hard-won wisdom, sometimes breaking into beautiful, lyrical language. *Remember you're here, please don't forget,* writes Kali. *Someday it will be your turn to rest but you don't get to choose. / You will know the time has come when the wind sighs its last / and the flowers weep petals for their loss.*

Every human has a story, and every story is valuable. Most of us would agree to that. What might be more difficult for us to agree upon is this: all of us, speaking in our own original voices, achieve at times literary art. It may not be published, but the artistry is there. The voice that Paule Marshall has called "the poets in the kitchen" and John Wideman has called "the voices of home" – the voice used at home with family, at the bar with friends, in the night with a lover – is in fact the first, primal, and universal human art form. Every person has it. It is a travesty that our educational systems and our artistic snobbery have fenced in "literature," excluding the majority of people on this planet from their own artistry.

What, in the most profound sense, are we doing, using the Amherst Writers & Artists method in Mary's Place and in other, similar programs in jails, prisons, shelters, hospitals, centers for youth at risk and many other venues across America and in Canada, Ireland, India, Malawi and other countries? It is true that we are changing lives. My own life was changed by a seventh grade teacher, by a college-age camp counselor, and by the pastor of a small, dying church. Each one of them dared to walk up the steps of a tenement through the smell of urine and roach poison, find me and believe in me until I could believe in myself. That is the "most profound" work being done in Mary's Place. Face-to-face, person-to-person, spirit-to-spirit, sharing words, stories – the "teacher/leader" writing with the participants.

Original Voices is not about literacy, although the practices that created it are crucial to the development and deepening of literacy. It is not about therapy, although its practices can be healing. It is not about educational theory, nor literary critique, though its goal is to revolutionize those.

The implications of our understanding and our practice are huge for the teaching of writing in general: first grade through doctoral studies, and in settings where writing is used as a method of empowerment or healing. We have gotten it backwards, and not just in America. I found, working in France and Japan, that it is a global quandary. Trying to teach writing, we instead teach inability to write. *Not being able to write is a learned disability*. It is taught by well-meaning teachers from about grade three through the Ph.D.

The core misunderstanding is this: The teaching of craft before establishing trust in the learner's own voice destroys the basis of writing as an art. We must first affirm, strengthen, and listen to *original voice*. Only upon the foundation of a person hearing her or his own voice and believing in its value, can we build a structure of craft. Original voice is the surest access to the unconscious, and the unconscious is the birthplace of art.

Are we saying "standards" don't matter? Are we saying "craft" in the art of writing is useless, or irrelevant? Absolutely not. What we are saying is that the teaching of writing must not put the cart before the horse. To begin to teach writing by insisting on the use of proper middle-class (or above) English, is to unintentionally teach that the language the learner brings to the table is inferior.

In fact, the "language of home" has already been somewhat established in the womb. We now know that a newborn recognizes the voice of his or her mother. Rhythm, cadence, the music of spoken and sung language already is known enough to distinguish voice from voice. The foundation of the writer is already laid. By the time a child is a few years old, he or she has mastered an enormous amount of craft: sentence structure, story structure, manipulation of language to express humor or outrage, and on, and on.

Original Voices gives readers an incredible opportunity to deal with some of our own prejudices about what is art, what is literature, and who are these homeless or formerly homeless women? *May you who wander, / writes Janet Backster, Never* be lost.... We are drawn close in their sharing. Renegade Amazon writes, *We have names! We are your sisters, mothers, daughters and grandmothers. We have names.*

Persons whose lives are impacted by societal or familial dysfunction receive a different kind of "education" than those who come from stable, supportive environments and sufficient prosperity to receive what we call "higher education." The very word, "higher" betrays our embedded hierarchical educational systems and practices. My brilliant young friend, R.M., writes out of her own experience of being stabbed while she holds her baby and is watched by her four-year old son. She is the age of my children. What she knows is very different from what they know, graduates of our countries best colleges and universities. The essential questions for us are these: 1) Is R.M.'s "education" (what she knows, what she understands, what she does not know, and struggles to understand) intellectually inferior to the "education" of those more fortunate? And 2) Is R.M.'s *original voice* adequate to tell her own story?

What would happen if we were to radically value the *original voices* of all people? Value them so much we are able to begin to enter the portal – narrow though it may be, "grammatically wrong" it may seem to us – enter into the experience, the life, it reveals? The music will be different from our own. The experience may be as foreign to us as that of the young mother, stabbed as her son looks on. R.M.'s development as an artist with words has to begin where someone values the wisdom of her experience and the articulation of her story in her own voice. As she herself learns to value those, she begins to want to learn craft. How to turn a passionate first-draft outburst of the essential facts of her story into a form that can even more deeply reach her reader. How to break lines of a brief vision into a sonnet or even a villanelle. She will want those skills, and a wise guide will offer them to her without in any way dismissing the power and integrity of her own voice, raw in her original drafts.

We are about *revolution in the way we understand art.* It is an outrage and a disgrace that our understanding of art is dominated by assumptions of class and privilege. That our definition of art in language is limited to the voices of those who have what we have deemed "higher education." Think of the voices in refugee camps, in housing projects, in inadequate schools or no schools at all. Think of the voices that have been through "formal education" and are silenced by Ph.D. committee critiques, by elementary school grades, by the *learned disability* of accumulated failure and shame.

It is deep privilege and a healing into family, to allow oneself to read, to listen to these voices. To imagine them gathered into a room, writing their truths, their stories, their poems. Brookland writes, *Scars. About face, / raw scars. / Not about ugly, scars. / About beautiful survival, / scars.* And Myrna voices, *As I write I create myself over and over again.*

Original Voices is about revolution. It dares to value voices that have not only been excluded from our definitions of literary art; they have been excluded from acceptance across all of the lines of ordinary human dialogue.

Pulitzer Prize winning poet Philip Levine youth was spent working in Detroit factories, which led him to speak for the working class in some of his writings. He has been widely quoted as saying, "I saw that the people that I was working with ... were voiceless in a way. In terms of the literature of the United States, they weren't being heard. Nobody was speaking for them."

This book leaps beyond even what Levine was talking about. As important as *speaking for them* might be, this book goes farther. Here, they speak for themselves.

– **Pat Schneider**, Founder, Amherst Writers & Artists and
Author, *Writing Alone and With Others* and
How the Light Gets In: Writing as a Spiritual Practice,
both from Oxford University Press

INTRODUCTION

About Mary's Place

On any given day there are more than 4,500 homeless families seeking shelter, help, support and safety in the City of Seattle. Each night, just over 500 families in King County are sleeping outside, in places unfit for human habitation - a car, a doorway, maybe a tent.

Mary's Place is a leading voice for homeless women, children, and families in emergency situations. Our work keeps struggling families together and provides practical tools and resources that help women find housing, employment, and stability. In addition to our day center for single women in downtown Seattle, we currently operate five emergency family night shelters accommodating more than 250 family members, and have recently opened a second day center in north Seattle, where we are co-located with other service providers to make it easy for families to get the resources and assistance they need to move out of homelessness.

Mary's Place serves hundreds of women and children annually, with over 40,000 visits last year to our day center alone, most of those women. Women come to Mary's Place for many reasons: a job loss or rent increase, a divorce or domestic violence situation, an injury or illness. On average, our women are 50 years old; the vast majority are dealing with abuse or mental health issues.

Women find acceptance, hope and dignity at Mary's Place. The day center in downtown Seattle provides a safe place for women to rest, build community, and find the resources they need to reclaim their lives: two hot meals a day, showers, laundry, clothing, medical care, and connections to housing, employment, and financial benefits. Discussion groups, classes, and on-site services contribute to physical and emotional health; crafts and community service events provide respite from daily worries. One of those programs that brings our women an opportunity for introspection, healing, and joy is Julie's *Write to Heal and Have Fun!* workshop. We are so grateful for her love and wisdom.

– **Marty Hartman**, Executive Director, Mary's Place

My Mary's Place Story

When I moved to Seattle in the summer of 2007 from the Midwest, my husband and I paid nearly double the price for a one-bedroom condo in Seattle's Belltown neighborhood than we paid for our four-bedroom home in Missouri. Sticker shock. And culture shock. I had never lived in a big city. For a while, I was disoriented, not myself – even depressed. In addition to experiencing all the usual adjustments after a move, my new neighbors included many homeless people, people who slept under the awnings of my building, people who carried their belongings in wheeled-carts sometimes covered with a plastic tarp, people who often had brown cardboard signs with words like: *Homeless. Hungry. Anything Helps. Will Work for Food or Money. God Bless You.*

I'm ashamed to say, at first, as I struggled to adjust to living in the city, I was so overwhelmed by the great number of people in need, by the smells of urine on the sidewalks, and people needing a shower and food, that often, when approaching someone who appeared homeless, I walked faster to quickly pass by. I avoided making eye contact. Slowly, as I adjusted to living in the city, I started purchasing *Real Change*, an award-winning weekly newspaper, which makes employment opportunities possible and takes action for economic, social and racial justice. I began to learn more about people in Seattle who were experiencing homelessness – what was being done – and not done, to address the great need.

I looked for ways to become more involved in my neighborhood. One evening I attended a Belltown Community Council meeting. Marty Hartman, Executive Director, other staff and clients of Mary's Place, all spoke. Marty is a woman with a smile bigger than the crescent moon, a woman who thinks possibility and solutions, an energetic woman with a big laugh, but mostly she is a woman who is love personified. I was touched by her words and the words of all the women who shared their stories that night. One thing Marty said, something I've heard her say many times since, was, "Come sit beside us."

That was something I could do. Maybe I could do more. But what? In the decades during my childcare and counseling career, I advocated for children, women and families. After moving to Seattle, I rediscovered another love of mine: writing and pursuing an education in writing. In 2010, I trained to be an Amherst Writers & Artists (AWA) affiliate. These two passions came together when I approached Marty at Mary's Place and asked, "Do you think the women at Mary's Place might like a weekly writing opportunity?"

She said, "Yes!"

Writing with the women, my neighbors at Mary's Place, has been a gift to me. I'm honored each week to sit beside and write with these women. They inspire me with their faith, hope and love. In their very being, words, stories, and responses to others, I see authentic, resilient, courageous, strong, fun, funny, intelligent, wise and creative women. I hope readers of this anthology will fall in love with these women and their words as much as I have.

–Julie Gardner, Editor

About The *Write to Heal and Have Fun!* Wednesday Morning Workshop

Write to Heal and Have Fun! began in 2011 at Mary's Place day center on Bell Street in a room off the large community room, a room with walls that didn't extend all the way to the ceiling. It was noisy, difficult to concentrate, write, and to hear women when they read what they wrote or when they shared their responses to what was read by another writer. Since 2012, after Mary's Place moved into the lower level of Gethsemane Lutheran Church, an increasing number of women have come to the writing table. We create a safe space for women to express whatever they want by strictly adhering to the practices of Amherst Writers & Artists.

Each Wednesday I arrive a little before 11:00 AM and open the door to what is always a lively, noisy place. Women are knitting, learning to write resumes, studying, drying their hair after a shower, reading, relaxing, visiting with others and eating. The scent of toast and coffee fills the air. After I make sure the conference room is available, a loud announcement is made, "*Write to Heal and Have Fun!* is about to begin." I entice women to participate by sometimes adding, "there's chocolate" or "in the quiet conference room." Though the room may appear to be chaotic, as it is often filled with donations, boxes of mailers and other items, especially during the holidays, it is quiet. The absence of noise is a welcome respite for the women at Mary's Place. Once we are seated and writing around the table, all the clutter in the room and from the stress of living falls away.

If a woman writes for six weeks, she receives a journal thanks to people who generously donate them. For a woman to be able to write six consecutive weeks is rare, due to work schedules and other life demands. Some have done this. I love the look of pride on a woman's face when she sorts through the box of journals to chose one that is perfect for her.

During the quiet writing times, we only hear the sounds of our own words and the etching of words onto notebook paper with pens. Sometimes a woman enters late or leaves early because she needs to take care of basic needs: showering, seeing the health nurse, or completing applications for housing or other services. Sometimes, on what is called "Bon Mary's day," a woman must go shopping when her number is called. Donated clothing, shoes, personal and household items are set up in another room. Women have earned shopping points. No one wants to miss their turn to shop at Bon Mary's for things they need and appreciate, so much so, it's like going to Bon Marché (now Macy's). We go with the life-giving and lively flow of the day.

After I offer a suggested prompt, we write for four to twelve minutes. When my phone's timer, the sound of a harp, goes off, women are asked to finish the thought they are on or to leave the table to continue writing. The women who remain at the table are invited to read some, none or all of what they just wrote. We listen. When a woman finishes reading, others respond. We use AWA guidelines, beginning comments with one of these three types: what I liked, what stays with me, or what is strong. The writer just listens. No criticism, suggestions or questions are allowed. To create a safe place to write, we assume everything is fiction and maintain confidentiality about what is written. This continues until everyone wanting to read has a turn. We write and read two or three times.

At first, we met for an hour, but as more women came to write, we increased the time to an hour and a half. Attendance ranges from one person to eight people with an average of four writing each week. Only once or twice in the past five years has no one shown up to write.

What happens in that room is far more than putting pen to paper: we share our stories; we write; we read; we listen; we respond; we laugh; and we cry. Often, we are surprised by our own words. We are: heard, witnessed, and connected to each other. Not so alone. Women have said, "This is better than therapy. How fun. Thank you."

We leave feeling better than when we came into the conference room, more in touch with ourselves as individuals, creative expressive beings, and writers – having had a positive community experience.

About This Book

The title *Original Voices: Homeless and Formerly Homeless Women's Writings* was inspired by Pat Schneider's foreword. We have seen every woman's creativity and heard unique voices from women who have a deep well of life experiences from which to draw upon, to contribute to the world.

When the *Write to Heal and Have Fun!* workshops started in 2011, we never imagined we would publish an anthology. Sometimes women's writings were featured on the Mary's Place blog and Facebook page or read at Mary's Place meetings and events. Some writers worked to submit and publish in a Women's Housing Equality and Enhancement League (WHEEL) publication, *The Occasional Times*. A few of the pieces included in this book have been published in *The Occasional Times*. This is how the file of writings began. With increasing numbers of women participating on Wednesday mornings, and with the support of many people who are recognized in the acknowledgements section of this book, the dream grew into a reality.

Most, but not all, pieces were written in Wednesday morning workshops. They are original first drafts written in four to twelve minutes. Some haven't been edited at all; others are lightly edited. More information about our editing and decision making process can be found in the appendix.

It is our hope that after you finish the book you will have a better understanding and appreciation for each woman and her writing and all of the Mary's Place women. We invite you to read the pieces aloud; maybe you will hear and feel some of what we experience in the conference room on Wednesday mornings when we are given and receive the gift of another's words.

was my furry 4 legged guy
who still waits on highway
101 - cars lay down for me -
I'll be going back next week for
my side kick -
No plan ner say -
So I may take a bath -
on this -
But thats like she loves
the water and she makes
and

Deep sea fishing is my favorit
thing to do we go The deep
In the ocen. Habit pls The
bottom fish and good to eat
Deep sea fishing 4

sticks & stones -
Along they speak too
these 1000 year old muses made
or pressed together pebbles and
or compressed layers by ages
centuries old -
I hold them in my hand and
ponder wence they come from -
Trying to glen some Ancient
wisdom of the silent ones
I heard one that in every stone
a rock is a soul and that being
Is Ancient and was living 100 or more
lifetimes than I that their
energy is just slower but their
one patient and if her a use
a mountain or hold a stone very
Quickly - you can hear & feel the
truth of ages - And wisdum
whispered -
I try to do that almost
every day - Usualy - something
crosses my path - something
And I bolt out like a squirl
like a boober - my sharle
squirl - on so much look
wisdum of ages - guess I'll
have you try again on my
next walk about -
nuts & squirls
squirls & nuts

I am a Phenomenal Woman

– Anne B

I'm not a beautiful woman, not of a model's measure.
Charisma has been my friend and brought the bees to me.
Which left me in wonder?

Someone once told me that my aura was red which means
I am warm with a good heart.
And I make people comfortable.
This is true.

I love to dance and the girls and I would dance in the middle of the dance floor.
Together we were and still are phenomenal women.
To this very day we still love to dance.

I've always been proud, honest and true, open-minded and take people at face
value.

I am a phenomenal woman.

* The prompt was Maya Angelou's Poem "Phenomenal Woman" from *I Still Rise* Copyright
©1978 Random House.

My Grandmother

— Leah

My grandmother is a phenomenal woman. She has raised 12 kids of her own, grandchildren and some great-grands. She has taught me to always look on the bright side. She was the only one in my family that would open the Bible and teach me things that would better myself. She would always warn me about many troubles in life. There would be many obstacles when you are trying your hardest, but stay focused on your goals. My grandmother made we want to learn and read and thirst for knowledge. I want to be strong like her.

* The prompt was Maya Angelou's Poem "Phenomenal Woman" from *I Still Rise* Copyright ©1978 Random House.

Before thing got complicated. Or so it
they were simple. ~~Its all relative~~
~~picking out paint color~~
Periwinkle could suit a boy
or a girl. Not oil-based as the
fumes were known to be
unhealthy for ~~a~~ a pregnant
women. ~~The Laura Ashley border~~
~~with Periwinkle background with~~
~~flowery script letters, also~~

choose a

Before thing got complicated ~~they~~
were simple. Or so it seemed.
Periwinkle could suit a boy or a
girl. Not oil-based, as the
strong fumes ~~were~~ known to
be unhealthy for an unborn
baby.
   She knew she would choose a
Laura Ashley border because it was
well. Laura Ashley. Simple, elegant,
preppy. Not outrageous, ~~or~~ risky, or
outstanding, the ~~little~~ of the white
colonial house w/ black shutters
and a swing ~~hung~~ from a huge
oak tree Shouted Fairfield City, CT.
   She sat the heavy wallpaper
book on her leg and slowly turned
~~each~~ pages one at a time.
Smoothly her fingertips across
~~every~~ textured ~~page~~ as if
~~that~~ ~~would~~ to reveal her choice,
Every page ~~as~~ insinuating a very
real possibility.
                    ↓ an edge of
                    something more to come.

Tone
complication
to tone

sound
b/c.
mood.

Never Liked, Always Liked

— Beth

I've never liked beets;
I've never liked to get whippings;
I've never liked cottage cheese;
I've never liked being abused;
I've never liked getting lied to;
I've never liked arguing;
I've never liked fighting;
I've never liked cold weather;
I've never liked being molested;
I've never liked seeing my mom murdered;
I've never liked being the only provider for A, B, and C;
I've never liked being in pain;
I've never liked separation for long periods of time;
I've never liked being alone;
I've never liked working 80 hours a week for 10 years;
I've never liked being cheated on;
but I've always liked my independence.

If I had Only Four or Five Lines Worth of Ink or Time Left

– Beth

how I pray,
how I asked God
to bring me, plant me
somewhere, I could be happy

Here I sit today
having been homeless for two months,
met a lot of amazing and not so amazing women and people

I've grown to love God and can
communicate with him
unlike I have ever been before
Thank God for himself and his son Jesus Christ

I care more about myself
I care more about my health
I know I can love and be loved
Without being hurt.

I'm glad I'm going back,
going back
with more wisdom and knowledge
than I came here with.
I learned
to humble myself

Life is important
Family needs you all the time
Relationships have complications
I am an overcomer!!!!

Never Liked, Always Liked

– Mary Ann

I never liked
Loud ministers, a screaming one screaming loudly,
A rollator with small wheels,
waiting for red light to turn green.
I liked Mom's stew, and cinnamon rolls,
fresh cooked salmon.

*Editor's note: A rollator is a walker.

Never Liked, Always Liked

– Marceline Jackson

I have never liked
public speaking,
being the only one on the dance floor,
living in the same house
with my relations in my
immediate family,
but the one thing I do like is
to go shopping for clothes.

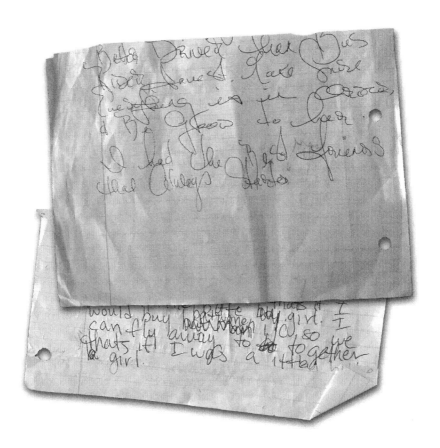

If I Had Only Four or Five Lines Worth of Ink or Time Left

– Marceline Jackson

I would write about how God has blessed me
and brought me through difficult times and hardships.
How he has lifted me to
believe that with God all things are possible
and to believe and have faith in God
and do not doubt him.

I want to instill that in my son
so he can prosper and
reach his goals in life
in his job search.
Allow him to find employment soon,
Keep him from all hurt, harm and danger.

Cherry

– Marceline Jackson

Cherry is one of my favorite flavors.
It is sweet and not too tart.
I love cherry pie and cherry snow cones.
Cherries are good for the heart, especially for women.
I picked cherries from neighbors' trees when I was a kid growing up.
It was a lot of fun.
I would take them home and my mom would make cherry pies.

* The prompt was a Starburst candy.

Rain Moves Over

– Marceline Jackson

Rain moves over the garden.
The garden blossoms and grows when it has moisture to irrigate it.
Beautiful flowers of all kinds spring up and decorate the yard or greenhouse.
The garden will not wither and rot when it is properly watered.
Rain is a very good source of irrigation.
It aids the watering of the garden done manually.
Rain is an essential tool to take care of a garden.
Rain produces healthy flowers and helps prolong the flowers in a garden.

Dove

– Marceline Jackson

Dove is a peaceful and loving bird.
It shows beauty
And is an object to look at
And visualize when you are in
Distress or an unpleasant situation.
Doves can help
Relieve tension and depression
When a scenario is written
Under the picture and is read.

Patchwork Altar Cloth

– Marceline Jackson

Patchwork altar cloth.
I like to crochet.
It is one of my favorite pastimes.
It is very therapeutic and fun.
One of my favorite patterns is the Granny Square.
I have just completed a blanket for my queen size bed.
It is nice.
After I complete the writing class
I will start on a new pattern.
It is for a friend of mine here at Mary's Place.
One of the staff here at Mary's Place
Will assist me in learning the pattern.
It is called an Easy Ripple Afghan.
I learned to crochet 8 years ago.
Since that time I have made
10 blankets for gifts for my friends.

Mean People Suck

— M. J.

Mean people suck.
My ex coming down off his crack high.
The lady who asked me to move my stuff
and she didn't like me standing behind her.
<u>Rude.</u>
The people who pretended to be my friend,
now want more and more money for storing my stuff.

It sucks to be me.
I had a stroke.
My body is in constant pain.
I'm unbalanced and it's hard to walk.
My equilibrium is off.
Extremely anxious going
Up and down stairs.
Shy to talk (used to be outgoing).
No teeth!!!

Don't judge me by how
I look.
I'm educated
I'm smart
I'm funny.

Oh Wondrous Day

– M. R.

Oh wondrous day unravel before me
My worries and woes
I drift aimlessly on my day off
First my needs, that right! Seeks my needs

Where is that place?
9th & Stewart
Oh! I'm hungry and thirsty. There's a Subway.
Wait there's a red door; is this Mary's Place
Down the stairs?

"Hello Mrs. R." She coordinates housing.
My daughter and my dog are on the streets.
Look there are clothes but I must do a chore.
Now I write to express my feelings, gratitude.

How wonderful a day in Grace!

Starbursting

– M. R.

I have an empty nest. I get to start over.
To do what my heart desires, to follow my conscious.
To burst upon the world with affect and brilliance!

I have nothing to hold me back. I am informed
And have access to know more…
I have skills, tricks and plans to activate
my dreams.

Now I just have to limit my dreaming; I want
to open a restaurant,
host a transitional shelter,
get help for the WHEEL program,
get married LOL
Starbursting is exhausting

* The prompt was a Starburst candy.

She

– Diana Balgaard

She, the tall, thin, and wrinkle free woman, lets me on the bus first. I would guess she is late 60s, early 70s. She appears ageless; her eyes twinkle as she smiles at me. Sitting on the bus, she stares forward not looking or talking. Her hand grips a metal shopping cart lined with a black plastic bag, two brooms neatly packed and covered at the top. Dressed in well-worn, clean clothes, and sturdy shoes, her hair is covered with a faded kerchief. I have seen this woman for years. She has been riding the bus for years, one of the homeless pioneers. She appears strong, agile. With perfect posture, she appears proud and confident. Is she covering or resigned to her life condition? I see no signs of inner turmoil, or unhappiness. Her cheekbones reflect the light and possibly her Native American heritage.

I study her and realize I could learn from her strength, her manner, stillness and peace.

This year they counted more than 3,600 people living outside, not sheltered. I would guess 4,000 because of ones they did not see. In such an abundant city, this is shameful.

I see huge rent raises shrinking me and others. There is no rent control in Seattle. The ones getting hit are the elderly and low-income. Thank your lucky stars for what you do have.

* *The Seattle Times* reported on January 29, 2016 4,500 people were sleeping outside in Seattle and across King County during the region's annual One Night Count. This is a huge increase from the figures of 2015 when Diana wrote this piece.

Her Body Moved
— Diana Balgaard

Her body moved and swayed to the music. It was as if she was wrapped in her own world twirling and jumping through invisible hoops with such grace and landing soundlessly on the wooden stage.

Her fingers appeared electric as she finished each position and routine–extending graceful digits of her fingers as they lengthened and finished the set–eager to begin the next movement.

Without stopping her body swayed constant joy as she danced across the stage.

Silence

– Diana Balgaard

Walking on the darkened wet
        sidewalk
        silence

Trees and plants
shimmering from the rain
rise in my sight
and pass me
as I walk in
silence.

Leaves dotted with
silver drops
left as tokens by
the cleansing rain
come into focus
silence.

Trees swaying in the wind
shaking away moisture
waiting
for the sun
silence.

Refreshing silence
permeates
my body with
a breath
lifting me to the
magic of
silence.

Meditation

– Diana Balgaard

In the direction of the sun I could see flowing waves of golden liquid entering my heart space, expanding and surrounding my whole body, accompanied by a penetrating, loving warmth and ecstasy. I wanted to stay here forever.

The sun moved above my head, then moved down my body highlighting eyes, throat, thymus, abdomen, knees and feet, scanning for tension and pain.

I felt only the sun and realized I was not this body. I was a sphere of crystal light.

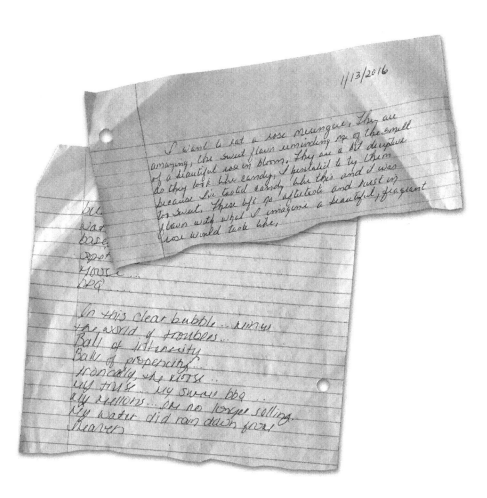

Aztec Indian

– Diana Balgaard

I the singer stand on high
On the yellow rushes
Let me go forth with noble songs
And laden with flowers.

Let me go forth as a new pioneer
burrowing into secrets
without any fear.
Let me go forth time traveling
Dimension to dimension
observing each Space.

Playing amongst stars
and places beyond.

Waiting for Earth to ascend
in heavenly waves,
she will take her place.

Turning and twisted, dropping
shackles of time
erasing the Chaos of humankind.
She waits patiently
for her appointed time.

* The prompt and opening stanza was a line read from
Ancient Nahuatl Poetry, "I the singer stand on high on the
yellow rushes; let me go forth with noble songs and laden
with flowers." Brinton, Daniel G. (2013). Library of Aboriginal
American Literature: Ancient Nahuatl Poetry, Containing the
Nahuatl Text of XXVII Ancient Mexican Poems (Vol. 7). London:
Forgotten Books. (Original work published 1890)

I Can't Elope

— Diana Balgaard

"I can't elope," Pepper said to the Cantaloupe. "Your size is intimidating."

Cantaloupe replied, "My orange color is for harmony and happiness. I am soft and juicy when eaten, and my hard exterior protects me against your opinions."

Pepper said, "I am spicy and bite the tongue with fiery lasting taste. I awaken the mouth with a slight burn. No one can forget me."

Blessing

— Diana Balgaard

May you be blessed with Sun and ecstasy on your path.
May you be blessed to shed your Armor, to show your true heart.
May you be blessed in pain in order to reach the light that blazes within,
waiting to ignite.
May you be grateful as an angel in flight.

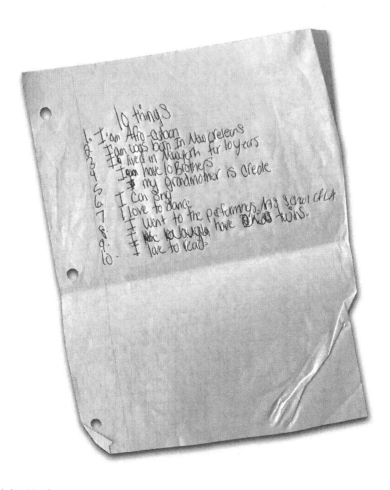

What I Need Today
– Diana Balgaard

This is what I needed today after weeks of being stuck in remorse of life undone, and feeling there is nowhere to go from here.

I love the beach white sand, sun and silence. I wasn't doing silence then as I do now because it magnified my loneliness.

My trails and adventures on Orcas Island: lived with rustic cabins, walking in deep thick mess. I was by myself all day and didn't mind. I remembered the magic I felt rowing in a boat, hearing only laps of water with each paddle, and water caught by the sun, looking at rocks and finding fool's gold, silica and agate with my little rockhound book and magnifying glass. These were a few treasures I can return to, only in memory.

The Moon with Dimples

– Diana Balgaard

The moon with dimples
Black sky of mystery
A sandbox for toddler creativity
The Penny Three
Sunlight discovers hidden dirt

Paper

– Diana Balgaard

I am writing to my best friend paper.
Paper,
I love you. You are like an addiction, drawing me to our welcoming pages, non-judgmental and open minded. Your beautiful, clean white space inviting clarity. You and me, we have a history of love, anger. Sometimes I deface you, pressing hard on your soft, gentle surface. You felt and absorbed the heat of my emotions like a trooper. You endured the tears, soaked as I blurred your lines. You never tore or weakened. But most of all, you were able to share with me loving words, beaming with light leaping from you into my heart.

My Mary's Place Story

– Angela Lugo

I don't even remember how I heard about Mary's Place. All I know is the relief I felt once I stepped in. It was quite wonderful to step into. I don't exactly remember my first day.

I keep coming to Mary's Place on a regular basis after leaving the overnight shelter everyday at about 6:45 and then I would show up at Mary's Place at 7:00 AM, opening time every morning.

I would then pick a table after a few minutes of unloading my things and collecting myself. I would then grab a cup of coffee. Then I would grab some magazines back when Mary's Place still had a great collection of magazines. *Vogue, People, Vanity* and whatever else.

Then there was always somebody to chat with. Every day someone new would come along and I would make several new friends at day, at least that's what it felt like.

Then, of course, there was community meeting which I have always enjoyed. Then my shower. Of course, followed by lunch.

Oh Mary, Oh Mary

— Angela Lugo

Oh Mary, Oh Mary
You're so not contrary.
Thank you for all the opportunities you've given me.
Thank you for all my sisters from all walks of life.

Childhood

– Angela Lugo

Childhood
Peanut butter and jelly
Perfume
A brand new start
Air
A fireplace
And a warm book
And good blanket
Friends
Playmates
Nostalgia
Crayons
School
Work
Daily
Nah! Nah! Nah!
Crayons, I could eat them.
They're so good.
A deserted island.

I Need Turquoise

– Angela Lugo

I need turquoise back and all its siblings and friends, back in my life.
I need to trust my therapist to (maybe help me to) put them back in my life,
in a positive way.

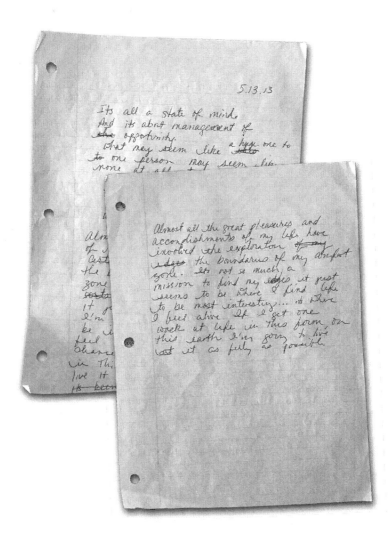

Through all the Gold

– Angela Lugo

Through all the gold
Here …
There were four apples on the tree,
red stained through gold,
that all might see the sun went warm from core to rind;
The green leaves made the summer blind
in that soft place they kept for me
with golden apples
sweet behind.

Exit 17

— Karli

When the sun shines down, down on this street, the peak of its rays shall surely reach across the striped black top and through reborn bushes to suddenly vanish.

Where shall you be when you finally see that your wheels have brought you to Exit 17?

Is there a hole in the grandeur small creatures lie?

Or a door propped open, reading and waiting for your arrival?

Will the leaves and branches part to reveal something magical, mysterious or dare I say murderous?

Or will the road continue on with no change?

When you finally reach Exit 17,

Will it be different?

Will something change?

Maybe your smile will be wider or your frown lower.

A new hitch may appear in your step, or your feet turn to lead.

Or maybe the new DOT guy forgot to stencil on details.

And it's another day like today in the end.

No matter though.

You're already here.

* The prompt was an image titled *Exit 17*.

Remember You're Here

– Karli

Remember you're here, please don't forget.
Someday it will be your turn to rest but you don't get to choose.
You will know the time has come when the wind sighs its last
and the flowers weep petals for their loss.
Wait for the sky's last blue.
Hold onto the ache of bones and strain of muscle.
Grip them as tight to your heart as you can hold them.
Someday you will be satisfied by the release of time.
Someday those darker days will make you chuckle.
Right now they make you cry.
Those tears will fill the oceans,
casting a stronger hue to the sky
So when finally your day has come,
the bluest of blue will greet you
and you will find you're taken by surprise.
All those aches have vanished,
the tears no longer fall.
To cast one's eyes on the sky's last blue
is worth the pain from it all.
Like the touch of a mother to quiet a child's cries,
so will the last blue lull you into sweet, sweet dreams.

From The Time I Woke Until Now

— Karli

I woke up extra early, hoping that somehow someway I would find myself on the other side of town before the afternoon. With help, I'd been given a quiet, secret place to stay for a few days. Unluckily, I didn't have money to go back to town.

Shivering, shaking, hoping my medicine would kick in and help with the fear of my own shadow that loomed over me each moment I was awake, I waited at the station. Surely there was a bus driver somewhere that would let me ride for free. I had too much to do in that particular area. There was also the fear of events reoccurring in the area that I was staying that had me hunched over, wide eyed and ready to snatch up the next transfer I saw.

My mind twisted and turned in its familiar loop of anxiety until: pop, I could feel my muscles relax; I could breathe again. Ms. Brain was still revved to full throttle but it wasn't being translated into fear, for now.

Then the bus pulled in front of me. Hands shaking, I did the only thing I could think of, I started to speak stumbling over my words.

"P-please, sir, ah-eh, I'm trying to get to the doctor, may I please ride for free?"

Over the past few months my mind has picked up on how many impolite folks there are in my life. I've forgotten that there are still people who care.

Small acts of kindness can sometimes be the only thing keeping me rooted to reality.

It would have been nice if the bus hadn't broken down half way.

* The title was the prompt.

I Don't Have Many Memories

— Karli

I don't have many memories of sitting at a kitchen table.

Many, not too fond, experiences have pushed the few memories of my early world to the side in favor of more negative thoughts.

Not wanting to dredge up those negative things just yet, I remember a hamster.

Our kitchen table took up nearly half the living room of a tiny two bedroom apartment.

Yes, we did use to eat there when I was eight or younger.

After that we took to our separate rooms – and televisions; something, should I have children, we will not do.

When the table stood empty for too long, taking up unnecessary space, was when we welcomed into our lives school project, Tetra.

My sister, the jealous type, had to have fish as well so she obtained goldies.

Now this may sound surprising but cats, rats, mice, fish and a hamster can all live under the same roof without becoming a mess at some point.

In fact, Marvin (Nickname Bubby) was very amiable with Spike, an adopted feeder mouse that had been jumped by his mates at Petco & couldn't be sold.

Bubby mourned his passing as I might a close friend.

When I think of the prompt, I think maybe something to do with your family and meal times.

To be honest my "pets" seemed closer to me than my family.

They didn't pick on me or tell me what to do.

We ate our meals together, different food of course, and they unconditionally loved me and took care of my needs as best they could, as I did theirs.

Someday I want that again.

Mom, I WILL be taking Fluffy back one day.

* The prompt was reading Joy Harjo's "Perhaps the World Ends Here" from *The Woman Who Fell From The Sky* by Joy Harjo. Copyright ©1994 by Joy Harjo. W.W. Norton and Compnay, Inc.

My Mom was a Drunk: True Story

– Karli

I can't think of a reason to change my name, no one, including my parents, gets it right anyway. I am: "Kayl, Kali, Kelly, Candy." Never my name.

Maybe it would have been more fun for my mother to allow my father to name me after his grandmother, Queen Elizabeth. Her name was a slave name. My name is from *Days of Our Lives*, but spelled differently.

She (my mother) was very lazy, she admits, when naming and raising me. I am the fifth child. My next of kin shares four out of five of the letters in my name. Hers has Hindi origins. Mine a soap opera. She is the one my mother readily admits she had put more effort into which has always made me question the paths, from childhood to adulthood, I have made, and if any of this knowledge helped to shape my current situation. If so, what could that mean for my future?

Yes, there is always your own will involved when it comes to decision making, but my will was shaped while being "raised" by her.

As I try to deviate from her path, I think of her telling me how she did the same with her mother. I'm led to believe many children do this.

Maybe I should change my name just to cut ties with that part of my life. I am honestly terrified of turning into her. Constantly Drunk. Seriously unhealthy, lazy, uninspired, never doing ANYTHING. Then I realize I lack the resources to get away from that option. The only way to change it would be to start down her path as my sister did: homeless with children. I could not bring myself to have a child in such an unstable environment. But I want – NEED – the bus tickets, clothing help, places to stay, in order to get a job and my own home. FUCK FUCK FUCK.

Once Upon a Time

– Elsie

Once upon a time there were two black ants that worked very hard to earn their living and managed to rise to the top in building their fortune. At the top of their successful life they decided to split their treasure between themselves. They had to use their sword to fight for their half ownership. Just as they began to fight they realized that it was not worth splitting what they worked so hard for. They put their swords together and became one in mind and soul and found their peace in greatness.

Lust Is...

– Elsie

Lust is a book under the bed which may be counted as a novel; some truth and imagination mixed with it as though it is equal to joy that brings to the heart, which may either at the beginning or the end, or even during the process culminate in trepidation, resulting into being an idol or a blessing.

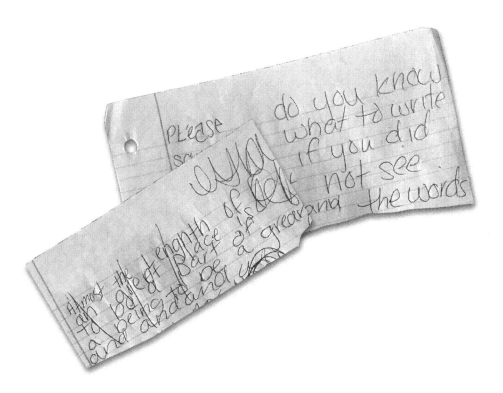

The Stick of Wood
– Elsie

The stick of wood looks like a snake. It may have once upon a time been a snake, which due to metamorphosis changed into a wooden one or the plant from which this stem had been broken from, must have taken the shape of the venomous animal that had troubled the life of the tree and those that were climbing it or were around it. Therefore, and then maybe, and just maybe when the part of the branch dried, it might have taken the hope of the deadly animal that ate the life out of the hook which had left a foreseeable mark for us that are sitting around this table on which the object of our writings lie (for those of us of who chose to write whatever has been revealed to us at this moment).

Quaking Aspen Leaves

Dedicated to Tina

– Jennifer Hamilton

Quaking Aspen leaves
quaking in my knees
my my
flutter by
memories on the breeze

These I've seen before
monuments
                    of the score
between life or death
        as the street life goes

And then I saw her
leaning back
Aglow....
Straight again
The wall
Chin tilted up
So often seen tucked in a
book
So deftly hidden
Not to show
how true and strong
she really is
Blessing a book of nouns
Blessing a mural of
life's cup

Alpha (and) Omega

– Maria

Alpha (and) Omega
       The First (and) the Last
The Beginning (and) the End…

       My friends as it stands, it is clear, that A
       (being the operative word)
       has the secret, hidden in our hands.
       The hour is at hand –
       The hands of the clock demands…
       chance to glance, to enhance
       Time and chance happen stance,
       And, And, And … meaning
       This (and) this … meaning
       quite possibly … the past is
       with present, and future … all right now …
       and … and … and …
       Time and chance is always
       at hand … closer in man …
       … fulfilling all plans.
       I stand with the first, last,
       Alpha, Omega,
       Beginning to End…

I Walked The Green Mile
— Maria

I walked the green mile…
My Emerald city's concrete piles…
Increasingly and extremely
terrifying … "I have to be dreaming."
Seemingly, interestingly enough…
arrived on the other side up
the tracks … Walls to my back …
Watched by the eyes of the
pack …
In fact … for a fact …
My life is back.

* The use of ellipses in Maria's writings was in her handwritten piece. They do not
represent words that could not be read by the editor or confirmed by the author.

The Past, Present and the Future Walked into a Bar

– Janet Backster

As the past, in the present, asked the future, "What would happen if I socked the past in the nose for not being present and accounting for the future?"

"Well," the future said "sure but the past, the present and the future are all one in the same, so better to buy a round of drinks, kick off your shoes and dance. Laugh a little."

The changeover from bliss is a much nicer hangover than a steak on a black eye.

And friends in the past will be friends in the present and make for a happy future.

"Have a nice day," said the present to the past who hugged the future.

And all went together smoothly from that moment. Everyone was very happy including the bar who smugly took credit for getting them all together.
As they say, Que Será, que será.

* The prompt was, The past, present and the future walked into a bar. It was tense.

J. P. Patches

– Janet Backster

While sitting on J. P. Patches street in Fremont, looking at Gertrude and J. P. Patches dance on an iron statue, I remember colors. Why did the artist use no colors?

Was Gertrude the first woman on TV in drag? And moose the golf balls? Or were they baseballs? No, baseballs would have knocked J.P. Patches and Gertrude out if they landed on their heads.

Oh the bubbles that popped and glistened on the TV screen and in my head as I watched J. P. Patches on my grandmother's black and white screen, all while the pitcher down the street at the Mariners practiced his spitball for the up and coming baseball game.

While J. P. Patches left the field, is now a stature forever immortalized: J. P. Patches Lane Freemont Washington, 52 years later, he still helps me smile.

Gertrude and J. P. Patches, though the artist forgot to do them in color.

My grandmother's TV was black and white.

In my memory I have color.

Blue Notes

— Janet Backster

Easy like water
Spilling
Falling Breathing
Ions in the Air Floating
Absorbing
Life's Kiss on the face
Like fine wine
The fall can be
Nice
When one is held and lifted
Like the note
E Sharp can lift you out of a
Low G note –
Though the lows can be a nice space
It lets you appreciate the
View of breath and the
Ruffle through your hair
And in between
When you're
Up high
On the E Sharp Realm –
You can play off
The G Note
And the Jazz
You're there –
No rehearsal
Just play –
One note
Then another
A wise man once told –
Go with the flow
Think I'll go with that
JAZZ

Blessing

—Janet Backster

May you who wander
Never be lost
and in the moment
be-knowing
You will always find your way
Our way;
And the we
in well–ness –
Putting the WE in front of
Illness makes it into wellness
That is what I wish for thee
To be in JOY at all of
Life's moments – to share
in the celebration of life
To celebrate your life
and live to celebrate with you.

To know the space
In between the words
is the breath,
and the words carry.
Breathe easy and sweet.
Kindness is stronger than
harsh words or swords.
Be kindness,
Receive kindness –
How sweet is this.
May you always feel
your heart beat as musical notes,
Your life the music.
May you know there is nothing
hidden to find.
It is there Always –
Be at peace & joy & at play –
No matter how you pray.

At Sixteen

– Janet Backster

At sixteen I believed in moonlight and magic –
Magic if you had a wart on your thumb
you could take an orange peel,
rub it on your wart
bury it under the full moon for three days
and it would disappear.
I tried it once after all else had failed.
I was mortified at school.
Of course it stuck out like Mount Rainier.
Made cracking noises –
Look at me!
Look at me so sensitive at sixteen –
I read somewhere that vitamin C if rubbed on a wart gets rid of it –
Magic or science – science or magic.
I suppose at fifty-two I still believe in magic and the power of the moon
though somewhere science came into play –
Somewhere along the way,
the two blended nicely,
though, for me,
The pull of the moonlight is just magical –
at sixteen or sixty-three.

Wish I Could Just Be Me

– Janet Backster

Wish I could just be me with my Dad. He keeps trying even when I don't take a Bath, which reminds me how I started this.

The guy at the smoke shop, when I asked, "Why does it smell so good in here, do you light incense?"

He said, "No! Do you know why it smells so good in here?"

I replied, "Why?"

"Because we take a Bath every day!"

For one on the street you wonder at the off sidedness and try not to take it personal.

What I do know is a Bath doesn't buy the Love or joy of a Dog – unless you've taken one in a River or Ocean with Side Kick, you wouldn't understand.

Dust Poem

– Janet Backster

Horton hears a Who comes to mind –
That whole tiny microscopic world
Whoville as contained on
One particle of dust –
Microscopic or at the least tiny particles,
Dust.
Dust carries spores I imagine and
other organisms that travel lazy
and soft to fall in the corners
under beds on tables and shelves.
Grateful I will be for a place and
A table to dust.
Those chores
Taken for granted or table tops,
Cherish them.
I will for it's
been many moons since I have had the privilege of collecting dust.
A rolling stone grows no moss and gathers no dust.
I like to roll, and then
I like to pause and take a rest.
It will be nice to dust my own table
And to collect dust
Horton hears a Who
And Janet does too.

Richard Bach
– Janet Backster

I still cry the floodgates
Still open - once in a while
I cherish those tears now
Much more than yesteryear
For they come less and less often
When they do they water the
Parched edges of myself
Prompting some long lost
Forgotten seeds to sprout
And bring forth life from the
Arid landscape of forgotten
Childhood - cracked, barren
Parched like a book I read once by Richard Bach.
He wrote *Jonathan Livingston Seagull*
And spoke of such memories
Meeting his child in
A field of parched earth
Cracked and forgotten -
A desert of lost childhood memories -
His child had a flame thrower and shouted,
How could you forget me!
When he called forth his inner child and opened that door.
My inner child hides behind
Narrow hallways peeking around
Saying "Do you remember me?"
You promised.
If I dared to open that
Door and ask little Janet
Is anyone home?
What would my inner child say?
Would my inner child come
Baring flame throwers
Asking angrily -
How could you forget me?!

A Flower in January

– Janet Backster

A flower in January?
The love bloomed in chill
and ice; for there is no
temperature that can cool
the warmth of that light.
Flower at will.

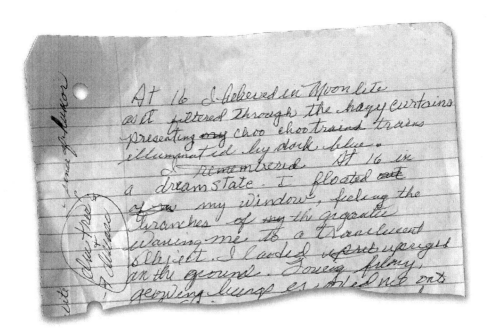

I Felt the Pores

– Janet Backster

I felt the pores in his nose
Big wet and shiny
Like his eyes – Full of joy –
My four legged God
Oh my! Did I say God???
I meant dog
Or did I…
(P.S. God is dog spelled backwards)
It also spells love –
Which is god backwards and
Forwards side to side and
Upside down –

Eulogy for the Fallen Women in Black

– Renegade Amazon

Today is a day of remembrance for our fallen sisters. The ones who died because our social systems are broken; funding that is continually cut. Prison systems that do not work, nor proper training programs to prepare us for the life on the outside so we do not have to resort to illegal activities to feed our children. Once you have that tale there are so few willing to give us a second chance.

How do we gain society's attention for those amongst us that need mental health hospitals so the street predators can no longer take advantage of those incapable of caring for themselves?

These are our numbers, we are not invisible, we have names. What happens to those that choose unwisely? Those who made the mistake of habit over habitat, the working poor. Who gave us a life sentence of living homeless on the streets to be humiliated, shunned and simply forgotten?

We have names! We are your sisters, mothers, daughters and grandmothers. We have names.

I am Unlearning

– Sue Johnson

I am unlearning the hypocrisy of our society, religion and my family. The questions I have asked several times to myself is, what is the success and what do we mean by "he/she is blessed and highly favored?" as many church folks ask. Is this success, I ask myself, and what really is this word in my vocabulary?

I grew up believing success is a happy family, a good job, a nice car, a beautiful big home, and friends, the dogs, cats, birds, rabbits, etc....

Since becoming homeless in Seattle, losing all my belongings, and the remaining ones stolen, I was left with nothing. My daughter has not invited me into her life and I often have those days when I ask the simple question: What do I learn from loss, and great loss?

Relationships are by far the hardest to lose. I would rather lose everything materially than lose a close family relationship. Well, I had to learn from even losing that.

I guess unlearning meant not to value any person or any material thing too much because they are not what define me as a person. Loss of people have been mainstays in my life, and to me, though it hurts badly, the loss of not seeing my grandsons, the attitude of my daughter does still bring big tears because I have not learned to deal with loss or abandonment. What do you unlearn about that? When I learned of the death of my dad that was easier than homelessness and the abandonment from my daughter. I stay pretty confused. If my mom was homeless and I had a house, I would put her in the bathroom if necessary. I'm unlearning trust. How do you really trust people, even people you raise?

We often compare and contrast what we learned in the past and what we know now. I don't really think it is unlearning as this is very difficult. It's far easier to learn something new than to relearn or apply new knowledge. I have had to do that since moving back to Seattle. All I can say is that though every day is difficult now, I do learn each day that success is really valuing who you are as a person and learning from others.

* The title was the prompt.

In the Direction of the Sun

– Sue Johnson

In the direction of the sun I could see the most spectacular ferryboat amidst the Cascades, Olympics and the blue water of the Puget Sound. I was in awe of the sky as it was all colors as the sunrise was gorgeous.

I had a rough night at a shelter and it was if the Lord said look above the hills, see the beauty and let it melt my heart. It did.

Despite the struggles of this cross-country move, the beauty here melts away the painful struggles and reminds me of the love of God.

The air is crisp and clean after a good rain. The flowers are in bloom and several shops have planters of every color flower imaginable.

I so enjoy the beauty of god and His great love for us. I see it every day in magnificent ways, just like today.

I can face tomorrow.

Achiever, Man of Worlds

– Sue Johnson

Achiever, man of worlds. I see this so ingrained in our society. Achievements that drive a person to the identity they want, work hard, strive for promotions, no failure accepted. The only problem with this is it so often kills well-meaning people. The man hoping to give his family all he wants to give them works twelve-hour days, seven days a week. The single mother trying to show her children how important achievement is goes the extra mile, spends time with her children, grandchildren and works seven days a week for that prize at the office – as in 2007. Three million dollars sold in real estate, meanwhile, the chemotherapy for breast cancer has to be fit in there also.

It's the American way, make a buck, work hard in your prime years or you will die in poverty. Work hard, go beyond what you can, strive to meet that sales goal, work hard to get all you can because, as life goes on, you hit a certain age, what can you do? Die alone in poverty. This is also the message given. Work hard to get that beautiful home, boat, camper, all you can because when you can't work again – then what?

Notre Dame de Paris

— Sue Johnson

Notre Dame de Paris early 14th century marble structure of Mary holding Jesus. Mary is depicted as elegant with a crown on her head and Jesus at her hip. This image is quite different from the "simple girl" Mary, a peasant woman at the mercy of society as she and Joseph escape Herod. Mary is depicted in this work of art as self-assured, confident and quite capable. She looks like an elegant princess with Jesus looking at her in awe of her strength and beauty.

My Intention

– Sue Johnson

My intention for 2015 is to secure housing, follow through on the hope of housing and to publish the story for children, pay all necessary fees to Washington Certificate and give myself time to do it because when I forgive my weakness and focus on what God has done in this journey, He will be my strength.

Mother Mary had unexpected miracles and I have also looked for a miracle in housing. The journey has been long and often confusing, as was Mary's, to be pregnant before marriage never knowing a man. Mary's first miracle was Joseph's protection. God honored her faith that what God told him through the Angel Gabriel that she was pregnant with the child that was the Son of God. She had no reservation that what she heard was truth. The Lord has promised me housing in Seattle as well. He has given me strength, healing and several good friends in this journey. Mary had Martha, while I have the people at Mary's Place.

The New Year is Coming to an End

– Sue Johnson

The New Year is coming to an end. The gift I received this year is to make the best of the journey. I made myself miserable during the first part of the year by asking, *How did this happen? Why did this happen?* I settled down and said, *Why shouldn't this happen to me, it's a part of life and even a way of life for some people.* It's just unheard of in my family. *So I set a new precedent,* I said.

I'm the first person to experience homelessness. I would rather say I set a precedent being an expert writer or anything else, really, however, in the journey of being homeless, I did learn more than I did in school, in college, in teaching school, and even growing up in a stable, secure family.

The journey of homelessness taught me to make the best of each day and it taught me what I used to jokingly say, *don't sweat the small stuff.* Really, you ask, "Homelessness is small stuff?" Well, a house is a shelter, a church offers shelter, and cars are for transportation.

Currently there are many Americans homeless, not the majority of them, however, many more than we want to admit. Job loss, medical problems, family divorce, or stolen money can all lead to homelessness. And homelessness does teach us: the small stuff is not our stuff. It's our way to handle the stuff as it comes.

You are What You Eat

– Tiffany

You are what you what you eat, I think therefore I am.
I heard somewhere, not knowing if this is true or not
But we all have nerve endings in our stomach that come from our brain.
When I heard this I started to wonder,
Does what I eat affect the way that I think?
Our thoughts have a tendency to shape
The world we live in.
If we think negative then a lot of time
Negativity will manifest outside of ourselves.
I wonder if that is the same for the type of food we eat?
If I eat something that is nourishing and has vitamins,
Will that make me have more positive thoughts and
In turn have more positive experiences outside of myself?
I think therefore I am.
I believe that often times, myself included,
We are not really mindful of the things
We put in our bodies when it comes to eating.

My Name

– Tiffany

My name was given to me by my mother but according to my grandmother she was the one who named me. She said she named me after the movie *Breakfast at Tiffany's*, a movie I still haven't seen all the way through but one day I will. I tend to lean towards my mother's version of how my name came to be; she said when I was born there were a few names she considered like Ebony and Africa. No offense, but I thank God she didn't name me after a continent. Then she said when she looked at me she thought that I looked like a Tiffany so that is what she named me.

My name is a Greek name meaning Manifestation of God. I love the meaning but when people hear the name Tiffany I think the meaning is the last thing they think about.

I always thought my name sounded like a valley girl's name or kind of superficial. As I got older I started to really love my name. Now, I think it is unique even though I had about two to three different Tiffanys in my classes when I was growing up.

Whether you call me Tiff or Tiffy or Tiffany, I do really love the name that my mother chose for me.

Thank God for Smashed Plums

– Victoria

Plums Plums
Plums. Smashed in my blanket
I forgot it and just forgot about it.
So it's okay.
Thank God.

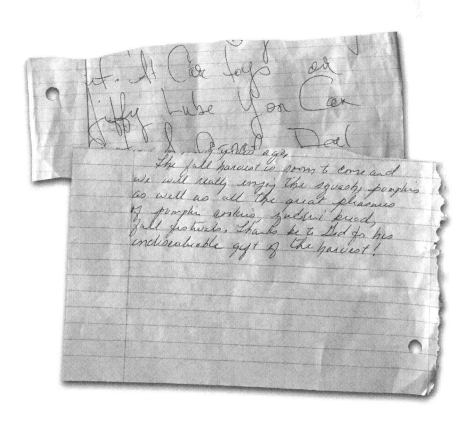

Where I Lived as a Child

– Victoria

      Where I lived as a child was a humble place with sisters, one older and one younger. Me, being the middle, of course. We were in very different growth and learning stages in our lives. They were the ones who climbed out of the window late at night while I was asleep in bed along with our parents. My older sister told me this story later in life. My response was how did I ever miss that? Fun, fun, fun. My parents never knew that it happened.

The Taj Mahal
– Victoria

The Taj Mahal reminds me of the Spike Lee movie, *Jungle Fever* with a family dealing with their oldest son addicted to crack cocaine, and the addicts would find a building and refer to it as The Taj Mahal.

Also people, a few I met on my journey have visited the beauty of the Taj Mahal.

This amazingly beautiful image, and I received a few post cards – one or two.

It's my desire to someday visit and take plenty of images to share in school and for others to enjoy.

Four Tools I Can't Live Without

– Pee Wee

GOD = created the universe, and everything in it.
AIR = which facilitates the intake of the vital minerals we need to sustain life.
FOOD = which supplies vital nutrients to our body.
LOVE = the common denominator which heals all wounds.

* The title was the prompt.

Men, Men, Men

– Kristine Bagby

Men Men Men Ha Ha Ha
The color of men
Rainbow. Ha Ha Ha.
United States of America
Man raised on the farm
with fresh milk
fresh air
best water in the state
My man.

Joy
— Kristine Bagby

Enjoying the kids while my girls can be kids.
Enjoying sunrises over Cascade Mountains.
What amazing joy
the sun would rise and at the same time
one by one the girls would wake.
Enjoy sunsets
remembering and hope for my children
and their children better days.
What a joy watching sunsets and Olympic Mountains.
Joy   Joy   Joy.

There are Many Artists

– Kristine Bagby

There are many artists.
Art is so much fun and comes in so many ways.
Art is in cooking.
After cooking the food, there is some art when a person can display food.
Veggies would be a good food that would be fun for displaying.
What about people that have no sight?
Well, for some there is an art of singing,
The art of singing from the soul.
Art is so much fun,
Beauty delicious.

Hands

– Kristine Bagby

Hands.
Strong hands.
My dad's.
Hands.
Mowing the lawn.
My man friend's hands.
With Holstein cows.
Sharing family – not just grandkids.
All kinds of hands are life.
Handprints of three girls.

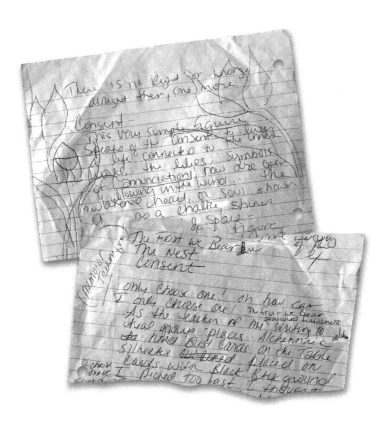

Cell Phones

– Kristine Bagby

Hello
Where are you?
Why are you there?

Who is this?
Why are you calling this number?

Hello
Meet me at the cell phone company

Cell phone contract
off account
on to a self account

Years later cell phone battle
Yes iPhone, Windows, Android

Communication
Cell
Phones

* Published in *The Occasional Times* Volume VIII, Issue 19 September 16, 2013

A Drive Down The Scenic Back Road

– Kristine Bagby

2016 Happy New Year
Driving down the back roads
Up to the pen
My how wonderful God is

Years later
Driving many roads
In town cars
Limos
Oh Yes
Remembering
Getting pulled over in Texas
By an Amarillo State Patrol Officer
In the stretch Chrysler

Easter morning
Oh how quiet the freeway is
In Los Angeles
On my way to church on Easter
Getting lost
Going back to North Hollywood
Ending up in Malibu
Listening to nice Jazz
Knowing I need to get back
To the holiday
In North Hollywood
Cali Easter 2007.

My Grandmother Told Me

– Pamela Herod

My grandmother told me to go out to the chicken house and collect some chicken eggs. She gave me a big basket with a towel inside. Her words were, "You better not break one egg."

She opened the door and out I went. I had never been to a chicken house. As I walked around her backyard I saw the house. Oh, the smell of it. I dropped the basket and started to throw up. By now the chickens were making all kinds of noise. And my grandmother said to me, "I be glad when you go back to Seattle."

Walking and Speaking with the Lord

– Pamela Herod

As I woke up one morning around 3:31 or something close to that I quietly slid off my floor mat to the sounds of 45 women sleeping. As I walked through the dim, all I knew, this was my time to say my prayers.

As I did, so I asked the Lord to take control of me today and let his will be done, among other things that was said. Walked over to the water cooler and took some sips of water. Walked back to my mat, giving thanks on my way back and lay down. When I woke up the thing I said to myself was *Lord we got to get up and get down to Third Ave to catch a bus so I can get to the SSI office before 8:00.* I remember in fast motion me putting my mat away. Grabbing my belongings quickly, so much so the night staff asked me, "Pam, what's the rush? I never have seen you move this fast!"

Since I've Been With the Lord

– Pamela Herod

    Since I been with the Lord, he has show me just what this little card says. When I was a three year old my adopted mother kept me in my playroom. I stayed there until she called me out. I kept these feelings inside me for many years until about two years ago. Lord has opened my spirit. Now, I can ask him for anything I need.

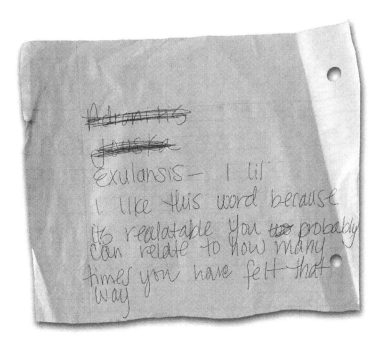

After Getting Out of a Relationship With Domestic Violence.

Inspired by James 3:17

– Pamela Herod

Despite the sexual immorality and violence of the present wicked system of things, we need to keep strict watch that how we walk is not as unwise, but as wise persons. And when disagreements arise, settle these without anger and wrath.

My Eyes are Gone
A Psalm

– Little Bit

My eyes are gone
I cannot see.
The way the world
used to be.
Where there once was so much light
I am saddened to say
There's none to find.
So help me Father,
I need your strength.
The darkness is vast.
And I am afraid.
For far too long,
I was lead astray,
But when I stumbled,
You still held me high
Even when I harbored so much
Hate
Through your eyes
I can see
the way the world
is meant to be.
Where there once was nothing to find
Now there is so much light.

I Hope the Stars Drip Down

A Psalm — Little Bit

I hope the stars drip down
And wash over me
To light up my soul
And set me free
I hope the stars drip down
And give me wings
So I can fly home
And be one with the breeze
I hope the stars drip down
to give me back to you.

Oh Lord, I Love You

A Psalm   – Anonymous

Oh Lord, I love you from the depths of my heart to the heights of my Spirit.
You are Lord.
My faith is steadfast.
Even when I struggle,
I know you are with me.

How Long God of Mercy?

A Psalm   – Avalon

How long God of Mercy, do we have to continually see the injustices in the streets, in homes, in shelters?

Where are you God of Grace?

I long to be your servant but I am seeking justice in your name.

Teach me to love like you see with your eyes.

For only in community can we thrive.

It is only in community that we can bring justice to an unjust world.

Help me serve You,

serve our community and

serve others in Your name.

Compassionate One, I long for you from the depths of my heart, to the heights of my Spirit.

You are my Lord my Rock and my salvation.

You are My Rock

A Psalm   – Avalon

You are my Rock and my Redeemer,
I sing a song for joy for you everyday!
I sit here in my mind so grateful for your Presence.
Big Hearted One.
You continually show me love, grace and hope.
I see You through the blues of the water,
the blooming of the flowers and
the care my neighbors give me
through it all.
Your love is everlasting!
It never leaves me.

How Long Oh Dear Jesus?

A Psalm   – Debra

How long oh dear Jesus
do we have to continually see the injustices in the street,
in homes,
in shelters?
Where are you now at this moment in my life?
I long to stay in the Spirit seeking justice in your name.
Teach me to be centered in my life.
I need patience so that I may benefit my community.
I need to remain in the Spirit.
Do not allow the Dark One to have the controls.
Teach me to divert his influence away from my life, so that I may serve God better.
In your Name dear God, Jehovah.

Justice Keeper

A Psalm — Sweet Justice

Justice Keeper,
I trust you from the depths of my heart to the heights of my Spirit.
You are my Judge, my justice.
Even when I struggle to know You,
You protect me.

MESSAGES FROM HEAVEN

1. Look up
2. Look around
3. Pay attention to sounds - clouds - Shining lights Abound
4. For this is God's GLOBAL GROUND
5. Messages From Heaven can be a positive rebound
6. A Pleasant day toward the Mountains
7. A Light through the darkness Pout
8. MOST IMPORTANT A PRAYER GIVING YOU
9. A RECIPROCAL MESSAGE FOR ALL WHO GLOBALLY
10. LET GO AND LET THE LORD HANDLE
11. YOUR DEALS, FEARS, TEARS, WEAR, DESPAIR
12. ANGUISH SPEARS
13. FOR HE IS MIGHTY AND WONDERFUL
    AWESOMELY PROFICIENTLY PROFOUND Just by his Sound!!

You are My Stability

A Psalm — Sweet Justice

You are my Stability.
I sing a song of joy for you everyday!
I sit here on my beach,
so grateful for your Presence, Father.
You continually show me love, grace, and hope.
I see You through the blues of the water,
the blooming of the flowers,
the care of my neighbors and my critter friends.
Through it all, your love is my joy and grace!
It never leaves me.

How Long Oh Protector?

A Psalm   – Sweet Justice

How long oh Protector,
do we have to continually see the injustices in the streets,
in the homes
in the shelters?
Where have you been?
I long to be your servant, but
I am seeking justice in Your name.
Teach me to use wisdom.
For it is only in community can we thrive,
it is only in community we can bring justice to an unjust world.
Help me serve You,
serve our community and
serve others in your family of Peace.

Yeshua

A Psalm   – Diana Balgaard

Yeshua, I embrace you from the depths of my heart to the heights of my Spirit.
You are my Guide, my parent, my light.
Even when I struggle, and can't hear or see You,
I feel you surrounding me with your Grace and Peace.

You are My Rock

A Psalm   – Diana Balgaard

You are my Rock.
I sing a song of joy for you everyday!
I sit here in your Mystery,
so grateful for your presence, Big Hearted One.
I see you in all of creation and the care you give my neighbors and me.
Your love is always flowing.
It never leaves me.

Everyone Knew

— Anonymous

Everyone knew not to go in there. It was dangerous. A place where people sometimes went in but never came out from. We were told it was because of the evil that lived in the form of the ash people.

Nobody knew much of anything about the ash people, and certainly none of it was fact, but the things we did know were enough to keep us away.

There was a rumor of a single person who had gone in and had lived to return. Everything we knew about the ash people had come from him in the form of an old, tattered book he'd put together but since then both the book and the author had vanished. Most of the people who had seen either were gone too. One day he'd be here and the next it was like nobody had ever known them in the first place. Because of this an entire book had been watered down to a single page, which we all had memorized a thousand times over.

- *You do not go into the nest of the ash people. You will die if you go in there. Even if you get out they will always find you. If you like living you will stay out.*

- *The ash people are not like us. They have empty eyes, empty souls, and empty stomachs. They are cursed beings who are never able to be satisfied no matter how much they are able to obtain.*

- *You cannot kill the ash people. They are nothing but shadows of humanity and are not living like us.*

- *They never leave the rest.*

They never leave the rest…. If only we knew how wrong we were because if we had then maybe, just maybe, we might have been prepared.

When I Was Young

– Hannah

"Not to put too fine a point on it, but you are damning yourself to bloody hell with that attitude." The dentist made no secret he was a devout fundamentalist Christian.

"Okay, if you want, spit." He left the exam room, and I felt it was all over – his tongue lashing, with me numbed up with Novocain trying to get past the fact I lost my first molar.

After all this talk, as I was exiting the office, telling them my insurance was covering the extraction, the dude came up, all smiles, holding out a tract like it was a thousand dollar bill.

"Lady, you cannot imagine how much I truly love you in Christ, but your attitude cannot help you to be on your way to heaven if you do not give up that dirty way of yours." He thrust the tract into my hands and turned on his heels.

I waited five seconds, and then gave him the bird.

The receptionist laughed. "Oh doctor, she has something to give you," the girl, a red-head with a bright smile, just rolled her eyes heavenward, and ducked down into a position so I could not see her.

"Miss Evans, what do you want to share?" The doctor seemed ready to eat me up so convinced he was he had redeemed a sinner destined for hell.

"Fuck you," and I turned to the door and vanished.

There was an Explorer

– Hannah

There was an explorer, who took trips down the White Nile, via the Blue Nile, and located a people who held that animal-gods could inspire men to find great truth. The *Indiana Jones* series of films had Dr. Jones, Indy, locating a temple in South America where extra-terrestrial, aliens from another planet had themselves in stasis as statures. A crystal skull Indy had recovered, awakened the aliens, and it turns out the temple was actually their spacecraft, which launched casting Indy aside, as he looked with great wonder at the event.

Truly, should nature, animals, bears, wolves, lions, elephants, even house cats and spiders, make an evolutionary leap, they may awaken something in themselves that connects to God. A rose by any other name is still a rose; and truth, however it comes, is made manifest, is still truth.

To Kill a Mockingbird began as a book written by a woman, who at the time was the personal assistant of Truman Capote, famous for his novel based on fact. *In Cold Blood* was the actual novel he was researching when his assistant showed him a draft of her book. Upon reading, he commented, "Is it for children?"

She said, "Maybe."

The film with Gregory Peck as Addison, the southern lawyer, father of two children he was raising alone, came across to the public as an iconic liberal, willing to defend a poor black sharecropper against the charges of rape of a white woman.

Despair in the south was never more finely drawn that in that film. Capote was narrow-minded. Rose – May – Call it like you will.

* The prompt was a quote from Rumi, "That which God said to the rose, and caused it to laugh in full-blown beauty, He said to my heart, and made it a hundred times more beautiful."

Making Strangers

– Mary

I met you years ago, our kids were friends first.
As time went on our friendship seemed to quench a thirst.
When you were in need, I was there for you unconditionally.
At times, when I was in need you tried to be there for me.
But now at the lowest, most desperate time in my life's journey,
Your true colors are shining and they look ugly and dirty.
I would think with all the years I've known you and been your true friend
Our relationship would grow stronger and better, not wither and end.
I thought when I met you I had made a life-long friend
But I guess making a stranger is easier than making a true friend.

* Published in *The Occasional Times* Volume VIII, Issue 16 August 5, 2013

As I Write I Create Myself

– Myrna

As I write I create myself over and over again. It's funny such a simple little goal can stir up so many different emotions, create different thoughts. How long did I live in a world where every day I could be something different to different people, so they'd never know how much I hurt, who I was, where I came from? My writing is exactly the same. Different places, people, some funny faces, some not so funny.

I could travel the world or look into a flower and see many wonders of curiosity, and then create my own story of that simple little flower and where it came from and where it's going.

Well anyway, I like writing and creating for that reason. Create, re-create, change a thought, be someone else. Change the world with one of your own. The choice is yours. Where will your thoughts and writing take you?

Home

— A.

Your household situation is improving through a move or healthy change in the occupants.

My experience with being homeless is very life changing. Not knowing how long the situation will last or if you will overcome it.

My life has not always been topsy-turvy. Before my papi got locked up I actually had a home in Long Island, New York. Where the grass was always shiny, birds chirping and sun always shining. Home was a home back then. Both parents, my siblings and I playing in the backyard climbing trees and swimming in the pool. That was the good life.

Now I am 22 years old looking for a place to call home. To find that happiness again. To have a peace of mind. I will soon get there, but until then, I dream about the years before and relive the experience and pray for it to come, come again in another lifetime.

Willingness

— Tonya

My goal for this season is willingness for myself
I am willingness
I go to people say *hi* and
Show myself as a woman
Not a low-grade person
Willingness
To show my light and humor
With all that listens to the Lord
I mean love good bad and great
Yes even the messed up
With all that I'm ok with
Myself because I'm very greatful
And loved by all
that's why I got – have a tattoo called
Loved by Liberty
Tattoo
You know
You matter because
You still live Love Lov Lo L

* The author's spelling of greatful was used.

Scars
– Brookland

About face,
raw scars.
Not about ugly,
scars.
About beautiful survival,
scars.
Not about pain,
scars.
About unexpected pleasure.
Not about serpents around my life.
About guardians true, too.
My life,
Now healed
are my
raw scars.

Decisions (Major)

– Kate

My body aches. I rolled out of bed. The pain was amazing. All over – what happened? Why now? The tears stung my eyes but would not roll down my welcoming cheeks. I managed to crawl out of bed. Slowly, I made my way upstairs. My body was taunting me, daring me to make it upstairs to the bathroom. I made it finally. After the climb, I was able to make it downstairs with less difficulty. This was the first day of my illness. That was the beginning of my homelessness this time. I did, then later on, make the decision to quit nursing.

I feel fantastic! Couldn't wait to get home, jump in the shower and go meet my friends for the evening.

Camp Long

– Anonymous

We played Red Rover
Cowboys and Indians
Cookware was our own can of Spam, especially my favorite.
Learning to cook on the fire was another favorite,
mostly because everyone had to purchase the special aluminum kit.
In high school going to Lake Chelan with my family,
I liked mostly because I would get away
by myself to swim in the indoor pool
while everyone at the place was outside.
This gave me an alone time
I'll always have.

Apples

– Selppa

How did the Creator decide
How an apple should taste?
How should the apple grow?
What color should the apple be?
Was he like a baker making several batches,
tasting his masterpieces?
Was he like a farmer who
studied the seed and
perfected the environment
to cultivate the perfect produce?
Was he like a blind man who
felt in his hands
what an apple should feel like?
Was he like a painter who
carefully picked his color palette and
hand painted the apple?
was he like the parent who
carefully named his creation?
Why apples and not selppa?

The Attic

– Jessica Jo Wood

I'm in the attic. The highest Place!
In your mind. The place you keep all
your historical monuments to your past.

I live there. There is only one key
to the door. There is only one way
to exit. The window is small and lets
the light shine in.

Will you come unlock the door
and set me free? Will you let
others know who I am? Will you
let me dwell in the other rooms in
your home?

I'm in the attic the Highest Place!

Strawberries and Apricots

– Jessica Jo Wood

The tickle, the taste of laughter.
Fresh strawberries sweetened with sugar.
Creamy, smooth, lustfully topped with Cool Whip.
Delicately moist, gently sweet shortbread.
Mmmmm. The taste tickles.
And the memories are always sweet.
Oh, but the apricot, it's deceiving.
It appears likes a peach, wet juicy, luscious in color.
Sweet at the first taste,
But turns into an ache as it's swallowed.
This ain't a peach mother.
My stomach curdled at the foreigner that just intruded.
Never again. I say, *Never again.*
But whenever an apricot appears on my plate, I eat of it.
This doesn't make sense.
There is something about the sweet turning bitter.
I wonder what it is?

The Patio

– Jessica Jo Wood

I can see you there inside the patio surrounded with glass.
You look out and see beauty.
I look in and see innocence.
She is trapped inside and unable to be free.
She is blinded by her own innocence.
I'm calling to you.
I'm telling you secrets.
I'm praying you hear me.
The windows are doors.
They have handles.
They can be opened.
Will you come out from your sacred place?
Will you grow into the woman I intend you to be?
Will you follow after me?
I have seen you gaze out the windows of my creation.
I'm setting you free now.
All your memories will return.
The windows are meant to let the light shine in.
Not to keep you a child forever.
So open the windows.
And be a queen.
And walk through with ease.
You were made for more than this.
Your patio will shatter one day.
So I continue to whisper to you day and night.

Bread Table

— Jessica Jo Wood

The dough is being pressed over and over.
Kneaded in preparation for the fire.
The dough is white, soft, stretchy and pliable.
The hand of the kneader appears,
pulls the large end of the ball of dough
up from the table,
stretching it one last time,
then kneads it together again.
Before, the dough was just flour,
had no form.
Before the preparation it was weak.
Now, it is helpless.
The hand of the kneader places the dough on the wood and sets it into the fire.
It bakes.
The sweetness fills the room.
The baker removes the bread and brings it to the table.
I was the dough being kneaded.
I am the dough in the fire.
Now, will I be the bread on the table too?
Will others enjoy the sweet smell of my scent?
What kind of bread will I be?
Will I be bleached and packaged?
Or, will I be whole grain, all natural, freshly pulled from the fire?
Will I continue to be warm from the flame?
Will I melt the hearts of those who dine with me?

Wars Have Begun and Ended at This Table

– Ms. Helena Rai

Wars have begun and ended at this table.
Broken down, screw by screw and even nail by nail.
The nails we used to support it again, after the previous failure to fix.
Broken down from forts and captains concurring the fortress be.
With a dance to shimmy on top of it to his victory.
Broken down, from the cat to the dog chase, and the cat always win.
Even a Doberman was no match for that shaggy green cat.
Broken down, from a car seat constantly dropping its top to parking.
From girls who witness teenage hood to motherhood synchronize.
Broken down, from indented circle ridges of …
From Dad's anger after work or gloat from Sunday football.
Broken down, from constant moving during construction.
Construction that turned the living room to the bedroom to the dining!!
Broken down, from photo albums to picture frames.
Memories of her scattered across it filling the room with laughter and tears,
A life too young to end.
Broken down, from sorting of old to broken clutter.
His goal was to get rid of the depression with every item.
Broken down, from loud music to careless feet.
From dancing with the new generation to the old Marvin Gaye.
Broken down in an Alley, just screws to wood,
Meaningless to the world but the center of hers.

Attic
 – Carla D.

The house was a three-story house with an attic.
At the top of the house there was a window for light.
There is a bed with wood floors.
It is empty
Yet I'm in the room.
Am I alive?
I'd like to explore this space.
The room is full of wonder
Yet all I see is a bed by the window on the wooden floor.
An antique style like French cottage Dutch.
I play, dance in the space
Yet I still look to one spot.
The bed is empty.
Are there sheets on it?
I wonder.
I constantly look for the window for light.
Where are the colors I wonder?
There is now pink spots I hope to place in object form.
Maybe pink hall?
Well that's too girly.
More towards yellow then that's too happy,
however blue teal white would be just right.
Has it been ten minutes yet?
What else can fill the attic with objects?
How about people and girlfriends?
A puppy to play with?
Now I'm in my shared room I grew up in with my sister.
Our new family's puppy is chasing us around
the wide-open space of the room.
We jump on the bed.

Resilience

– Carla D.

My word is resilience, just for today.
I pray Jesus that we may be resilient when resilience is called.
What does a resilient person look like to a child?
Who is a person at times of resilience?
When are we called to be in our most resilient state?
How I long to be resilient at a moment
when the pressure is heightened
and people are watching.
This has me thinking
a while longer that
to try to put one piece in front and
turn it to make sense.
The word rhymes with silence
and our sense of hearing
could be in check.
Is this a sign to check and listen
Deeper,
I wonder the word resilience
And a you
Re added with the
-ence is tense.
Does this make any sense?
Awaken your sense
To silence, quiet, peace, past tense, relax, made tense, rest.

The Music

— Red Rock

Music stirs in my bones.
I love the pitch.
I love the tones.
The creativity it entices brings me joy.
It carries out the tune like a newborn boy.

Creativity's cry can never die
Like freedom's ring and the love it brings.

For God so loved the world
He gave his only begotten son;
For only Mother's sweat and blood
Can forgive and forget what we've done.

Our child's song
We love and adore
I pray thee well
Go and sin no more.

I love you, Jesus Mother Creator

Goodbye

– Red Rock

Tears fall down my face
Like the train behind my door
They fall in my disgrace
Like blood staining the floor
What I did I just don't know
Downhill I slip like a slide on icy snow
What happens next
I know too well
My feelings mixed
I feel like hell
I told them not to worry
I pleaded with them to wait
I told them I was sorry
It was just too damn late
I opened the door
Then let it close
As one last tear
Fell down my nose
I said, "Good my friends…"
Goodbye.

The Picture

— Red Rock

The beautiful picture on my wall
Holds so many hopes and dreams
Inside that frame it looks so small
Yet that world is more real
Than it seems
Sometimes I think I'm really there
Usually that gives me such a scare
In that beautiful picture
Of mysterious wonder a world exists
Where there's no chance of surviving
I can already hear its mighty thunder
Calling me into a glistening pool
Of answers to questions I'm asking
Keeping signature on the banks
Of memory lane
I will always have this picture
Embedded in my brain
It's waking from a nightmare
Into middle earth
It's like giving the love of your life
Rebirth
In that dream world of love
I just cannot resist
I find myself floating above
All the pain in this world's
Foggy mist
And I find myself in its depths.

I Go Down to the Edge of
— Myrtle "penny"

I go down to the edge of,
Sanity, calmness
Sometimes it's not by choice
It just happens.
I met with an individual trusting me,
telling me how she really is adjusting to
the realm she may be in.

A deeper feeling of caring comes over me –
This person's trust, honesty and bluntness,
bringing into the light, the situation
how it really is –
My thoughts how could she speak
so lightly when she is
making sense of what needs to
be a complete turn about
And the wonderful law that is embedded deeply in my mind
If two would agree, it would
Be.

There needs to be change.
No more edge.
Edges hedges
Doors pledges
Promises, pleas
What about me?

Have I given or
Just expected
Have I shared
Or rejected?

What's the outcome
Has it helped some?
This minute this space
O God, may there be Grace.

What's the verdict?
Who's the judge?
Who do we contact when we're at the edge?

Campfire

– Myrtle "penny"

Oh, wonderful thought.
Just brought back wonderful moments.
My youngest child, Larry Wayne.
This is the year 1981-
These years KKK was in full authority in some states.
I was attacked by an Afro-American man.

You see truth.

Since the Lord protected me and brought me out of a truly horrible situation
I traveled wherever He sent me.
And being myself, let many, all see and know how awesome He is
What He alone did – in a sad sad time.

So had my way in the highways and byways.
I, too, was a victim.
By God's grace I came out of it alive –
yet down the road of time - discovered I was with child.

When the wonderful son was born I didn't tell all doctors –
So when he arrived – shock of attitude and disgust was in all hearts and faces.
I witnessed in a matter of minutes doctors, nurses completely changed.
They said when they brought Larry Wayne to me
This is your newborn going on three months.
This is in Galveston, Texas.

I had nothing for him.
Took him out of the hospital using my coat and a blanket.
Woman owning a hotel invited me to her home.
KKK called her, said if she didn't remove me at once they would burn her business.

Yes, we had many campfires,
By one-and-a-half he knew how to carry sticks.
And we had many wonderful times with a campfire reading the Bible –
Awesome time of my life.

My Own Fall Song

– Myrtle "penny"

As I'm walking thru – all the leaves that have fallen
Beautiful gold, green, brown huge leaves
Smiling like a child –
Not only because they are there
But I am, happily, not a worry, with no fear.
Sky may have a hint,
Maybe soon it will snow.
The sweet noise I hear and see
Are robins and blue jays.
And crow is singing.
Sparrow, quietly peaceful watching
And flying ever so quickly too far up for me to see
It's either hawk or eagle
Wonderful weather, is light, sweet
Quiet breeze.
Blessed thoughts
And sweet awesome moment.
Thank you
Happy Thanksgiving
Beautiful Kindness
Compassion

Home made Resume

– Myrtle "penny"

Home made Resume

1960 to 1970 ,-----was given signed over to Italian man , with four

Daughters.. ages 4,5,10,11.. with them for ten years

Worked... SINGLETON   shrimp factory...sort . packed, and machine work

        In a cigar factory.. shaded. Packed ,, boxed

    At Tampa   General Hospital.. ward clerk , for pediactrics

    Owned produce stand.. bicycle shop .. sold used cars..

This is all in Tampa Fla.

1970-1990

Worked in Chicago..Ill.

SPEEDY bowling alley,,,waitress., two years

,MARRIOT ,---BREAKFAST WAITRESS---maybe a year

Jewish restaurtant,,,, COLES , bartender,, maybe two years

1990

Got cancer........operation...removal.. recovered

Received GAU,, TO SSI TO COULDN"T WORK

2015

WORK IN CARNIVAL. PAYSON ,ARZ.

                    FOOD WAGON..COOKED.. CLEANED.. CASHIER

                    9AM TO SOMETIMES 1 AM

I AM A 71 YEAR OLD WHITE FEMALE

As you can tell very basic on typing and computer

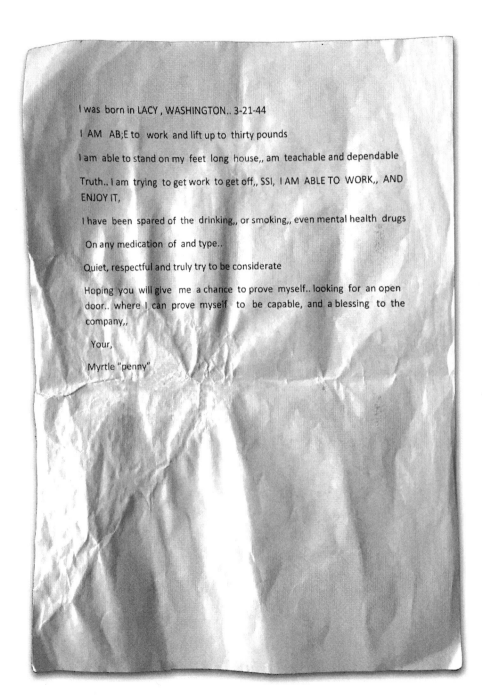

I was born in LACY , WASHINGTON.. 3-21-44

I AM AB;E to work and lift up to thirty pounds

I am able to stand on my feet long house,, am teachable and dependable

Truth.. I am trying to get work to get off,, SSI, I AM ABLE TO WORK,, AND ENJOY IT,

I have been spared of the drinking,, or smoking,, even mental health drugs

On any medication of and type..

Quiet, respectful and truly try to be considerate

Hoping you will give me a chance to prove myself.. looking for an open door.. where I can prove myself to be capable, and a blessing to the company,,

Your,

Myrtle "penny"

My Immortal Love

— LJ

I feel your presence outside of my bay window knowing you are in the shadows watching me, planning the night you will take me away to your castle over the waters.

Where we can safely watch the sunset over the mountains covered with snow and green trees. Me in your arms, you holding me close to your heart as our hearts beat as one with the same rhythm.

Your scent is so sweet and warm, full of loving like a rose in the morning, but yet not so innocent like a virgin who's never been touched.

Your skin, so soft like velvet on the rose that just bloomed, but yet so cold as death.

I know that the day you come into my room you will show me passion and companionship of all eternity. And we will both be immortal lovers that stay in the shadows watching the innocents.

Thanks to New Beginnings in My Life

Thanks to New Beginnings in my life I have grown over the years and learned: boundaries, love, sadness, lust, lost, and betrayal.

I learned that when you put your mind to it you can do anything your heart desires, and not give up. I have been betrayed in many, many relationships with family, friends, and lovers of all sorts of sizes and personalities, all sorts of forms, and walks of life on this planet.

I was in lust and love all at once and it ended me up in a lonely place in my life that no one dares to be or seek.

From all of my past relationships I have learned boundaries in my own life and personal space as well as mentally and physically. I know what I can and can't allow and how far I can go.

Now I have a new beginning to life. I go to school. I set my limits on boundaries. And I go to work. I'm on track to finding my permanent home. And I'm saving money. All of which is positive. I even changed my friends and places to hang out.

My Hands
– LJ

I look at my hands to see the aging, of becoming older in this lifetime. They are wrinkled and dry. They have scars from past fights from a younger more rebellish teenage. My nails are worn from biting out of nervousness. They are spotted, if you look close enough. Just another reminder of aging and getting older.

They hurt nowadays from sprains and broken bone, broken from work and horses as well as playing sports. But, yet, even though they are old and hurting, they are still strong and working.

They swell every now and then, but they still function in many ways from helping to exploring and writing. They wave hello and goodbye. They even tell you where the sun don't shine, if you anger them.

They still play piano and guitar. They make beautiful music – if you ever listen.

They tell the story of a young rebellish lady who has grown into an elegant and not so rebellish young woman.

Blanket

Dedicated to my Grandma

           – LJ

The color resembles the purification and innocence of a baby being born in a world unknown.

The design reminds me of an elderly woman who has lived her days up until the end, who has all sorts of stories she can tell you about a beautiful, meaningful life of struggles, heartaches, betrayals, survival and of the innocent fun times as a young child. Growing up, she was living a rough life, as a young woman, but she still survived all that was becoming of her.

Now, she is back as an innocent little girl, who is now with her Heavenly Father where there is no hurt, no struggle, and no betrayal at all.

Innocent love and purity, just playing in the clouds with the angels and her loving father.

* The prompt was a white crocheted baby blanket.

A Window
— Kathryn

A window has many stories.
For me it is about how clear a window is for the person looking through it.
…

Liberosis — I like this word
because I desire it. ~~to Because~~
Because I'm going though
so much. Right about now
as I ~~decided to~~ am writing
~~this down.~~

Story from a Story

Walked up a hill carrying a heavy backpack. I had gathered rocks. The pack was SO heavy. Threw the stones. One was resentment; one was anger; one was forgivingness. The pack was lighter. I could not see my blessings; I could not see beauty as I walked; I could not see the mountains or streams of waters. The rocks kept my attention on pain.

Forgot my backpack at the bus stop. Left it as I was thinking of many things. My lost husband, my runaway child, my lost money, my almost unpaid for house taken from three months of foreclosure ten days before auction.

Well the bus backtracked to get my rain soaked bag – found before it was taken. A miracle in itself.

Too many things to think of.

Now I want a puppy – one I can't lose.

A Man Gave Me a Dog

– K. O.

A man gave me a dog.
He asked or told me that the dog was given in his will to me.
He committed suicide.
We went to the pound to get the dog.
It is a security animal to protect me.
I am low income.
I feed the dog Pedigree®.

My No Good Terrible Bad Dog

– K.O.

My no good terrible bad dog.
Forgot my paperwork.
Papers of jubilee.
Papers of freedom.
Papers of appreciation.
What do I do?
Well, I've forgotten these papers many times.
Forgot my keys.
Where are they?
Where could they be?
They have to be close.
Where did I see them last?
Found security.
Into my apartment.
Keys on the bathroom door.
Lost my letter of encouragement –
found a copy.
Lost my debit card.
Did you find it?

Baby Blanket

– Beebe Berhe

When everyone is born they're wrapped in a white baby blanket.
We all start out life in the same way.
Some babies grow up in a great family,
others grow up in chaos, and
some babies grow up in a combination of both.
We need not forget,
when life gets wary, that
we all started the same,
wrapped in a white blanket.

It Goes Away

– Beebe Berhe

Life goes away as fast as it comes.
Children grow,
Flowers wilt since time has begun.
We look back at pictures amazed at our images,
Which were long ago,
Doesn't seem so long ago.
So as we take another breath
Tomorrow,
Let's remember,
Whenever life ends,
Life just started a day ago.

I Was Born into a Big World

— Beebe Berhe

I was born into a big world
Born into the unknown
I wish I was warned about the storms
But I had to discover them on my own
Learning to be optimistic in the middle of chaos
Sometimes not created by my own self
The child in me still feels like it's a big world of wonder
Because that's what I originally felt
Though my vision has fallen short
I still find joy I own

* For the prompt, we read "The Winter of Listening" from *House of Belonging*. Copyright ©1997 by David Whyte, published by Many Rivers Press.

Life is
– Little Bit

Life is
Movement.
Moving here.
Moving there.
Moving to.
Moving from.
Moving forward.
Moving back.
Moving
for the sake of
Moving.
But I think
that sometimes
It's okay to
just sit,
Think,
And remember
What
Exactly
We
Move
for.

Dear Reader

– Little Bit

Trust me
When I tell you
Life is hard
But it's worth living
Sometimes you'll
Fall down
And break your heart
In half
But in the end
You'll be stronger than before
And you'll know yourself
Trust me
When I tell you
You can't
Find happiness
If all you do is
Look for it
You have to create it
From the dust
Trust me
When I tell you
Not to judge yourself
Too harshly
You're only human
Less than perfect
And every once in a while
You'll fail
And that's okay

In Another Life

– Little Bit

In another life
I might have been
A superstar
Who wore
Expensive clothes
Was loved by most
Except myself

In another life
I might have been
A scientist
Who knew
The world was round
But didn't know
Happiness

In another life
I might have been
An athlete
Focused on winning
Unable to see
The truly important things

In this life
I'm just a girl
Not a superstar
A scientist
Or an athlete
But I love myself
I am happy
And I see that's
What counts.

It was with the help
of God my Lord and
Savior and the
belongings I had
been carrying with
me and despite
my physical
handicapped lengthy
shower at Mary's
Place helped heal.

Write for
to
Heal group.

For So Long I Did Not Have a Voice

– Jennifer Hamilton

For so long I did not have a voice
Trampled and broken I was silenced.
Like so many of us.
It may seem a small thing but,
You heard.
I feel so grateful
From my depths I thank you.

ACKNOWLEDGMENTS

My deep gratitude overflows to so many for so much, especially to:

All the women who have written during the *Write to Heal and Have Fun!* sessions for the past five years. You have kept the workshop going with your presence, shared writings and responses. This book and so much more would not be possible without you.

Marty Hartman, Executive Director of Mary's Place, for her loving leadership and "Yes!"

Mary's Place staff and board members, especially: Liz McDaniel, Erin McKay, Abbey Laninga, Kristi Tollner, Linda Mitchell, Zaneta McQuarter, and all the current and past front office and floor staff and volunteers who have supported *Write to Heal and Have Fun!*, this anthology and the women, children and families at Mary's Place.

Former Mary's Place Chaplain, Rev. Monica Corsaro, for her collaboration bringing the women's Psalms to this book.

Melissa Trull, Annette Peizer, Christianne Balk, Kali Wagner and Diana Balgaard, for stepping in to lead workshops when needed.

Annette Peizer, who deserves a huge and heartfelt acknowledgement. In addition to writing with us in the workshop for over thirty Wednesdays, she provided valuable feedback and substituted for me on some of those days, and she trained to become an AWA affiliate. Some of the writings included in the anthology are from prompts provided by her during the sessions she led. Additionally, she helped compile and proofread the manuscript. Most significantly, her unbridled enthusiasm and belief that the women's writings should be published helped turn a file of writings into a book.

Karen, for generously sharing chocolates and other items on Wednesday mornings.

Annie Lusk, who in her former role as Women's Housing Equality and Enhancement League (Wheel) Organizer, welcomed and published pieces written by women in Wednesday morning *Write to Heal and Have Fun!* workshops.

The AWA community, especially to founder Pat Schneider, who made all this possible in so many ways; Mary Tuchscherer, Jan Haag, and Chris DeLorenzo who trained me to be an AWA affiliate; Mary and Jan for their support and guidance in the creation of this anthology; AWA affiliates who trained with me and other AWA colleagues and friends; and finally, to Bridget Bufford: For years in her *Creative Writing of Columbia* workshops using the AWA method, she helped me to take risks in my writing as I developed my voice.

Mary Tuchscherer and Sue McCollum, for making it possible for me to go with a group of women to Malawi, Africa for nearly a month on a VoiceFlame, voiceflame. org, cross-cultural journey. We wrote with and led AWA workshops with girls and women throughout the country. There, I observed in others, something I have experienced and continue to experience – healing and empowerment through writing. These girls, women and my fellow journeyers inspire me and are with me in spirit as I write with the women at Mary's Place.

Sue McCollum, Elie Gardner, Sue Abare Gritter, Pat Schneider, Lane Goddard, Sue Walker, Maureen Buchanan Jones, Karen Buchinsky, Annette Peizer, Linda Mitchell, and Elizabeth Corcoran Murray for carefully proofreading or editing the manuscript or parts of it.

My dear writing group members and friends: Arissa Rench, Elizabeth Corcoran Murray, Kristine Forbes, and other writing colleagues and friends: Jennifer Haupt, Ingrid Ricks, and Jan Vallone for listening and brainstorming with me when the anthology was just an idea, for reading and making comments, and for all your support and love.

My Spiritus Dei spiritual community and book club: Sheila and Jack Mattingly, Marilyn Cass, Linda Mains, Linda Ware, Louise McAllister, Bev Coco, Jeanie Robinson and Jan Vallone. You have loved the women of Mary's Place and me through your presence, prayers and generous donations of time and resources, including journals for the women writers.

Writers in community-based WritersGathering, writersgathering.com, and Legacy Writing workshops and retreats who made generous financial donations to pay for the cost of this anthology: Ori Artman, Brooke Hall, Steve Giliberto, Janet Fisher, Patty Tackaberry, Elizabeth Coppinger, Arissa Rench, Nancy Bradburn Johnson, Amy Barnes, Kayce S. Hughlett, Susan Adler, Louise McAllister, Bev Coco, Jan Eisenhardt, Sharon Richards and Kori Lynn.

Last but not least, words aren't enough to acknowledge my family: my deceased but with-me-every-day parents, my brothers, sisters, their spouses and children for helping me to learn and practice unconditional love as we embrace each other, our commonalities and differences; my children and their spouses who have encouraged me to go for my dreams by living into their dreams; and my husband John for his unconditional love, support – for being a hero and role model in my life.

– **Julie Gardner**, Editor

APPENDIX

Our Editing and Decision Making Process

There has been little editing beyond spelling and some punctuation and even then, not in every case. Punctuation and spelling was not corrected when the original seemed to better represent the writer's conscious or unconscious intended meaning. At times, the writer used inventive spelling creating new words. Regarding punctuation, sometimes conjunctions have been added or omitted for purposes of clarity.

Since most of the work was in handwritten form, some words have been difficult to identify. Words that could not be identified are represented with an ellipsis. In a few cases, ellipses were part of the writer's format.

The formatting of the writer was used. In some cases, when the format wasn't clear in the written word, it became clear as the writer read her piece.

The title the writer gave was always used. When titles were omitted, the first word, phrase or sentence became the title, unless there was a strong word/line in the piece that highlighted the writer's creativity and writing.

At times, the prompt that inspired the writing is noted. When published works or lines have been the inspiration, every attempt has been made to reference the authors and sources.

Many women did not want to publish using their name for various reasons. The shame women feel, or worry that their family and friends might feel, especially when they first experience homelessness, is often overwhelming, and there are safety reasons. A few of the pieces have been written by women who have not experienced homelessness, women who come to "sit beside" and advocate for their homeless sisters. In all cases, the full names of women were not used, when women who gave Mary's Place permission to use their writing, were unreachable to approve the final edits of their writings and to confirm their bylines. Writers chose to use their first name, first name with a last name initial, first and last name initials, a pen name, street name or their legal name. Every writer included in this book will receive a free copy of *Original Voices*.

Every effort was made to protect the identities of people referred to in writings, sometimes changing the author's name or names in the piece.

In most cases, we chose to arrange the pieces by writer so readers could see and hear the writer's unique strengths and voice. Some women have more pieces than others because their attendance has been more regular. Every woman who submitted a piece has been included. These pieces are a small fraction of the thousands of Wednesday morning writings and some longer prose pieces brought in for feedback during the past six years.

APPENDIX

About Amherst Writers & Artists

Amherst Writers & Artists, AWA, amherstwriters.com, is an international writing organization founded on the belief that everyone is a writer. AWA supports confident and emerging voices through an established workshop method. AWA offers regular training for writers to become AWA affiliate workshop leaders who affirm this commitment in every workshop, with novice writers who have been led to believe they have no voice or with experienced writers who want to hone their craft.

Pat Schneider, the woman, writer, poet and editor, and founder and director of AWA for thirty years, in *Writing Alone and With Others*, Oxford Press (2003), offers a manual on how to write alone and with others. It's more than that, more than an outline of the practices, and more than the "Five Essential Affirmations" and "Five Essential Practices" outlined in the book and below. For me, the book and writing for years in an AWA workshop changed my life and career focus. I read Pat's work whenever I need to remind myself about what matters in writing – and in life.

For readers who may be interested in learning more about AWA practices, I encourage you to read the book, find an AWA workshop in your area and participate in training for workshop leaders.

The Five Essentials Affirmations

1. Everyone has a strong, unique voice.

2. Everyone is born with creative genius.

3. Writing as an art form belongs to all people, regardless of economic class or educational level.

4. The teaching of craft can be done without damage to a writer's original voice or artistic self-esteem.

5. A writer is someone who writes.

The Five Essential Practices

1. A nonhierarchical spirit (how we treat writing) in the workshop is maintained while at the same time an appropriate discipline (how we interact as group) keeps writers safe.

2. Confidentiality about what is written in the workshop is maintained, and the privacy of the writer is protected. All writing is treated as fiction. At all times writers are free to refrain from reading their work.

3. Absolutely no criticism, suggestion or question is directed toward the writer in response to first draft, just-written work. A thorough critique is offered only when the writer asks for it and distributes work in manuscript form. Critique is balanced; there is as much affirmation as suggestion for change.

4. The teaching of craft is taken seriously and is conducted through exercises that invite experimentation and growth as well as through response to manuscripts and in private conferences.

5. The leader writes along with the participants and reads the work aloud at least once in each writing session. This practice is absolutely necessary, for only in this way is there equality of risk-taking and mutuality of trust.

www.marysplaceseattle.org

Made in the USA
San Bernardino, CA
25 March 2016